von
Dr. Steffen Brand
Paul Dennis
Bärbel Hafner-Wünning
Silke Krieger
Christine Meißner
David Roberts

Anna Schönbach
Prof. Harald Sonntag-Weisshaar
Reiner Verspai
Bernd Wick
Dr. Christine Wieckenberg

Green Line

Oberstufe

Workbook

Ernst Klett Verlag
Stuttgart · Leipzig

So lernen Sie mit dem Green Line Oberstufe Workbook

Hauptteil

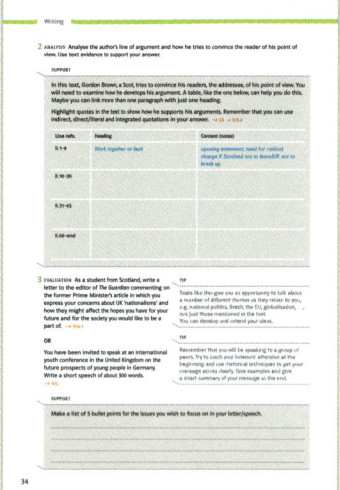

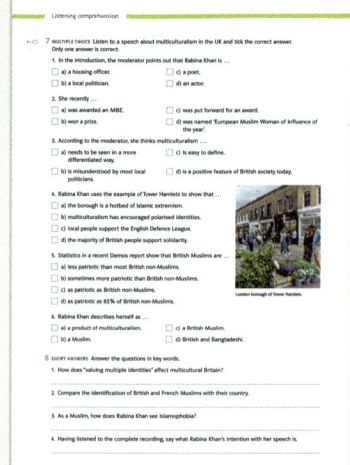

Kompetenztraining mit Aufgaben wie im Abitur: *Reading*, *Writing*, *Listening*, *Mediation* und *Speaking* zu jedem Topic

Nützliche *Support*-Aufgaben, *Useful phrases* und Tipps helfen Ihnen bei der Bearbeitung

Alle Lösungsvorschläge und Workbook-Audios sowie Transkripte finden Sie in der Mediensammlung zum Workbook

Übungsaufgaben vor jeder Klausur und nochmal vor der Abiturprüfung

Abi revision – Ihr Kurs zum kompakten Üben vor Klausuren und kurz vor dem Abitur

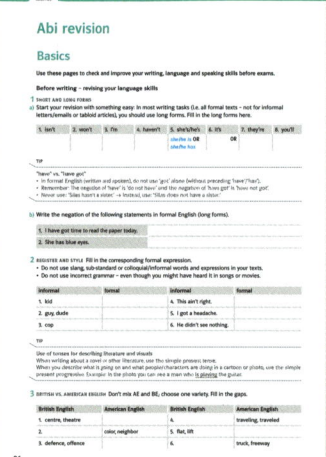

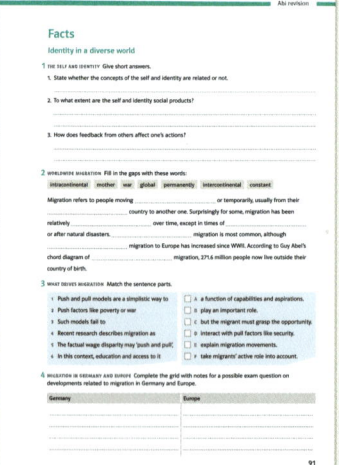

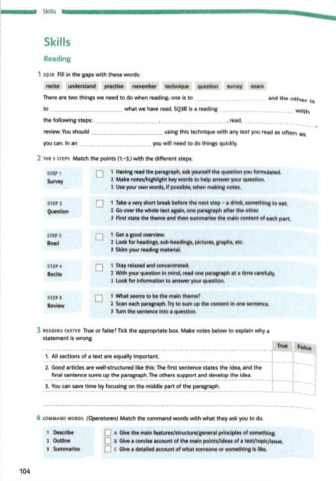

Die *Speaking*-Aufgaben können Sie alleine oder mit Partner üben.

Basics
Die wichtigsten sprachlichen Mittel und Stolperfallen: Selbstcheck und Übungen zu *Language* und *Grammar*

Facts
Kompakte Wiederholung und Übung des wichtigsten Faktenwissens zu jedem Thema

Skills
Mit diesen Tipps und Übungen können Sie alle Aufgabenformate sicher bewältigen

Symbole und Medien

👥	Partnerarbeit
A1 🔊	Verweis auf Audio (in den Medien zum Workbook)
→ S14.1	Verweis auf Skills im Schülerbuch

Abkürzungen

adj	adjective
AE	American English
BE	British English
e.g.	*exempli gratia* (Lat.) = for example
i.e.	*id est* (Lat.) = that is
infml	informal
n	noun, substantive
sb	somebody
sth	something

Die Inhalte der Mediensammlung können Sie online oder in der App aufrufen:

Medien zum Workbook:

🔊 Audios
Zudem enthält die Mediensammlung die Transkripte und Lösungsvorschläge.

So geht's:

1. Auf **schueler.klett.de** registrieren
2. Nutzer-Schlüssel oder QR Code einlösen
3. Digitale Medien online nutzen oder in die 📱 **Klett Lernen App** laden

🌐 Nutzer-Schlüssel
MU5f-mKzi-gf2U

Tipps für die Vorbereitung aufs Abitur

- Finden Sie heraus, welche inhaltlichen Themen und Aufgabentypen in Ihrer Abiturprüfung vorkommen können.
- Nutzen Sie die Tabelle zur Planungshilfe; üben Sie dann gezielt die inhaltlichen Themen und Aufgabentypen mit den vorgeschlagenen Materialien aus diesem Arbeitsheft.
- Üben Sie auch darüber hinaus mit weiteren Lernmaterialien, Originalklausuren und englischen Zeitungen sowie Audios und Videos.
- Planen Sie genügend Zeit für diese Übungen sowie 2–3 zusammenhängende Abitur-Übungsprüfungen ein.

Markieren Sie **Themen**, die in Ihrem Abitur vorkommen können!	Aufgaben in diesem Workbook zur Übung und Wiederholung	Zeitplanung Erledigen bis …
☐ Identity, gender and migration	Identity and migration in a diverse world ☐ Topic ☐ Abi revision: Facts	☐ _____
☐ Personal aims, social relationships and work	Choices in work and society ☐ Topic ☐ Abi revision: Facts	☐ _____
☐ The media and citizenship	The media ☐ Topic ☐ Abi revision: Facts	☐ _____
☐ Society in the UK	Tradition and change in the UK ☐ Topic ☐ Abi revision: Facts	☐ _____
☐ English as a lingua franca	The Englishes ☐ Topic ☐ Abi revision: Facts	☐ _____
☐ Society in the US	The US – a diverse nation ☐ Topic ☐ Abi revision: Facts	☐ _____
☐ International relations	International relations ☐ Topic ☐ Abi revision: Facts	☐ _____
☐ Postcolonialism, other English-speaking countries	India, Canada and New Zealand ☐ Topic ☐ Abi revision: Facts	☐ _____
☐ Global challenges	Global challenges ☐ Topic ☐ Abi revision: Facts	☐ _____
☐ Climate and ecology	Ecological challenges ☐ Topic ☐ Abi revision: Facts	☐ _____
☐ Science and the future	Science and visions of the future ☐ Topic ☐ Abi revision: Facts	☐ _____
☐ Shakespeare	Shakespeare ☐ Topic ☐ Abi revision: Facts	☐ _____

Markieren Sie **Aufgaben**, die in Ihrem Abitur vorkommen können!	Aufgaben in Abi revision (Skills) und in Workbook-Topics	Zeitplanung Erledigen bis …
☐ Reading comprehension	☐ Skills: *Reading* ☐ *Comprehension-* und *reading comprehension*-Aufgaben in allen Topics	☐ _____ ☐ _____
☐ Analysing non-fictional texts	☐ Skills: *Analysing non-fictional texts* ☐ Nichtfiktionale Texte in den Topics, z.B. *Tradition and change in the UK, Global challenges*	☐ _____ ☐ _____
☐ Analysing fictional texts	☐ Skills: *Analysing fictional texts; Analysing a scene from a play* ☐ Fiktionale Texte in den Topics, z.B. *India, Science and visions of the future, Shakespeare*	☐ _____ ☐ _____
☐ Writing	☐ Abi revision, Basics ☐ Skills: *Writing an argumentative essay; Writing a a comment on a non-fictional text* ☐ *Evaluation tasks* in den Topics	☐ _____ ☐ _____ ☐ _____
☐ Listening	☐ Skills: *Listening* ☐ *Listening comprehension*: alle Topics	☐ _____ ☐ _____
☐ Mediation	☐ Skills: *Mediation* ☐ *Mediation*-Aufgaben in allen Topics, insb. *Choices in work and society, Global challenges*	☐ _____ ☐ _____
☐ Speaking	☐ Skills: *Working with images/oral exam* ☐ *Speaking*-Aufgaben in allen Topics, insb. *The media, The Englishes*	☐ _____ ☐ _____

Green Line Oberstufe
Workbook für Baden-Württemberg

1. Auflage

1 ⁵ ⁴ ³ ² ¹ | 2025 24 23 22 21

Alle Drucke dieser Auflage sind unverändert und können im Unterricht nebeneinander verwendet werden. Die letzte Zahl bezeichnet das Jahr des Druckes.
Das Werk und seine Teile sind urheberrechtlich geschützt. Jede Nutzung in anderen als den gesetzlich zugelassenen Fällen bedarf der vorherigen schriftlichen Einwilligung des Verlages. Hinweis § 60a UrhG:
Weder das Werk noch seine Teile dürfen ohne eine solche Einwilligung eingescannt und in ein Netzwerk eingestellt werden. Dies gilt auch für Intranets von Schulen und sonstigen Bildungseinrichtungen. Fotomechanische oder andere Wiedergabeverfahren nur mit Genehmigung des Verlages.

Autorinnen und Autoren: Dr. Steffen Brand, Grünkraut; Paul Dennis, Lahnstein;
Bärbel Hafner-Wünning, Ebersbach a. d. Fils; Silke Krieger, Castrop-Rauxel; Christine Meißner, Panketal;
David Roberts, Salzgitter; Anna Schönbach, Speyer; Prof. Harald Sonntag-Weisshaar, Bisingen-Zimmern;
Reiner Verspai, Rheinbach; Bernd Wick, Neckartenzlingen; Dr. Christine Wieckenberg, Hamburg

Entstanden in Zusammenarbeit mit dem Projektteam des Verlages.

Umschlaggestaltung: normaldesign GbR, Schwäbisch Gmünd
Satz: media office, Kornwestheim
Druck: Gebr. Geiselberger GmbH, Altötting

Printed in Germany
ISBN 978-3-12-550014-3

Inhaltsverzeichnis

Section	Page

1 Identity in a diverse world

Text	8
Writing	9
Reading comprehension	11
Listening comprehension	12
Mediation	13
Speaking	14

2 Choices in work and society

Text	16
Writing	17
Reading comprehension	18
Listening comprehension	19
Mediation	20
Speaking	22

3 The media

Text	24
Writing	25
Reading comprehension	27
Listening comprehension	28
Mediation	29
Speaking	30

4 Tradition and change in the UK

Text	32
Writing	33
Reading comprehension	35
Listening comprehension	36
Mediation	37
Speaking	38

5 The Englishes

Speaking	40

6 The US – a diverse nation

Text	42
Writing	43
Reading comprehension	45
Listening comprehension	46
Mediation	47
Speaking	48

Section	Page

7 International relations

Mediation	50
Writing	51

8 India

Text	52
Writing	53
Reading comprehension	55
Listening comprehension	56
Mediation	57
Speaking	58

9 Canada and New Zealand

Mediation	60

10 Global challenges

Text	62
Writing	63
Reading comprehension	65
Listening comprehension	66
Mediation	67
Speaking	69

11 Ecological challenges

Writing	70
Listening comprehension	70

12 Science and visions of the future

Text	72
Writing	73
Reading comprehension	73
Listening comprehension	75
Mediation	76
Speaking	78

13 Shakespeare

Text	80
Writing	81
Reading comprehension	83
Listening comprehension	84
Mediation	85
Speaking	86

Abi revision

Basics

Before writing – revising your language skills	88
Preparing for evaluation tasks – writing an essay	89
After writing – checking for mistakes	90
Speaking – tips for oral exams	92

Facts

Identity in a diverse world	93
Choices in work and society	94
The media	95
Tradition and change in the UK	96
The US – a diverse nation	97
India	98
Global challenges	99
Science and visions of the future	100
Shakespeare	101
The Englishes	102
International relations	102
Canada and New Zealand	103
Ecological challenges	104

Skills

Reading	105
Mediation	106
Working with images – oral exams	107
Writing a comment on a non-fictional text	108
Analysing non-fictional texts and writing an argumentative essay	109
Analysing fictional texts	110
Analysing a speech	111
Listening	112
Analysing a scene from a play	113

1 Identity in a diverse world

Diversity in top jobs will benefit the whole of society

The author of this article, Doreen Lawrence, is a British Jamaican campaigner. Her son Stephen Lawrence was murdered in a racist attack in South East London in 1993. Doreen Lawrence has founded the Stephen Lawrence Charitable Trust which supports young people from disadvantaged backgrounds.

A traditional approach to nurturing talent is needed for a modern workforce. For far too long, executive positions in both the private and public sectors have been the preserve of
5 white males.

I therefore welcome the interventions by Sir Peter Fahy, who leads the Greater Manchester Police, and business secretary Vince Cable that we need greater diversity in important positions
10 across the country. Sir Peter's call becomes more urgent when you consider that only six chief officers in the police are from non-white backgrounds. When writing to the seven FTSE 100 companies that still do not even have
15 a woman on their board, Dr Cable made it clear that people from different backgrounds bring with them fresh perspectives.

A lot has changed in the 20 years since my son, Stephen, was murdered but a lot more
20 needs to happen. The UK will only reach its full potential when everyone, irrespective of their background, truly believes that they can make it. The Stephen Lawrence Charitable Trust is working hard to bring about this change.
25 The evidence shows there is still not enough diversity in senior roles. Research has found that even those people from black and minority ethnic (BME) backgrounds who manage to get jobs in professional occupations can often
30 struggle to progress up the career ladder despite suitable qualification and experience. In 2010, only 4.1 % of directors in FTSE 100 companies came from ethnic minority backgrounds. Statistics show that black university graduates
35 can expect a 24 % pay penalty after they leave university.

This is not only a British problem. In the US, only 13 black executives have ever made it to the top of a Fortune 500 company. Only six of them
40 are currently active.

While we welcome Sir Peter's understanding that it is important to have more officers from ethnic minority backgrounds, we have found that the vast majority of black people do not want affirmative action. They, and other ethnic 45 minorities, want to work in environments where they are assessed on their merit, rather than having people believe they only secured their jobs because of the colour of their skin.

We need to examine what gets in the way 50 when people try to succeed on their own merits but are not as successful as they would have hoped or their paper qualifications would suggest. They may not have the confidence to believe they can do a role. They may not even 55 aspire to a specific profession in the first place. They might be the first person they know to have "made it", which means they will not have the in-built network that their peers may have grown up with. And sometimes they will look at an 60 industry, not see anyone in it who looks like them, and decide to walk away from it.

It is not just about getting into a job in the first place. It is also about how people are supported to stay and progress. I have had 65 plenty of people tell me how difficult and excluding they found the culture of their workplace. They have told me that they felt overlooked for promotion and worked extra hard to get to where they are. 70

This situation is far from satisfactory, but we can change it. Historically, the Stephen Lawrence Charitable Trust has focused on supporting young people from disadvantaged backgrounds into careers in architecture; this 75 was what Stephen hoped to achieve, so it seemed like a natural starting point. We now plan to expand this model in order to support talented and driven young people from disadvantaged backgrounds into other 80 professions, too, including law, finance, medicine and media. The "Magic Circle" law firm Freshfields is to be the first major employer to partner with us. Our approach will involve supporting young people at the beginning of 85 their career with a scholarship: establishing a lasting relationship that will mean there is a rich talent pool of candidates for top jobs long term.

The trust is also developing a consultancy offer
90 to provide businesses with practical strategies to
build a diverse and more inclusive workforce.

Some senior figures pointed out that
encouraging diversity has important benefits.
It is in everyone's interests to make it happen.

Doreen Lawrence, *The Observer*, 2013

---

1 to nurture to foster • **3 executive position** an important job as a manager of a company or organisation • **4 preserve** domain •
6 intervention to get involved in a situation in order to help • **14 FTSE 100 companies** 100 companies listed in the London stock
exchange • **35 penalty** *here:* disadvantage • **39 Fortune 500** ranking of the 500 largest companies in the US •
45 affirmative action the policy of making sure that a particular number of jobs are given to people from minority groups •
47 merit ability • **69 promotion** to move to a more important job or rank • **86 scholarship** money given to sb to help pay for
their education • **89 consultancy** an offer to provide advice

→ To practise closed reading comprehension tasks, go to tasks 4–5.

1 COMPREHENSION Sum up Doreen Lawrence's article.

SUPPORT

1. The SQ3R method you have learned in your Abi skills section on reading can help you pre-structure
   your summary. You can formulate your questions here and then answer them on your own or with
   a partner. The first question can give you some orientation.

   • *What does Doreen Lawrence call for in her comment?* _____

   • _____

   • _____

   • _____

   • _____

   • _____

2. Now read the text again and answer your questions.
3. Write your summary. Do not forget to provide the context of the article (author, source, date, topic)
   in your first sentence. → S13

2 ANALYSIS Analyse the language Doreen Lawrence uses to convince the reader.

SUPPORT

1. Highlight words/phrases in the text that make this text a comment. Look for emotional language
   and personal statements aiming at getting you involved and persuaded.
2. In the left column of the table below you find two re-written sections of the text. Compare them
   to the original. Highlight the changes and copy the original from the text. Then analyse the effect
   of Lawrence's original word choice.

Re-written section	Original	Effect
1. […] Stephen Lawrence passed away 20 years ago and a lot has changed since his passing, but a lot more needs to happen. The UK will only reach its full potential when everyone believes they can be successful. […]		

2. [...] Many people find the culture of their workplace difficult and ostracising. They also complain that they felt overlooked for promotion and put in a lot of effort to get where they are. [...]

_____   _____
_____   _____
_____   _____
_____   _____
_____   _____

3. Match the persuasive techniques with the correct definitions and give examples from the text with line numbers.

expert opinion • repetition • facts and statistics • parallel structures/parallelism

- Persuasive technique: Definition:

_____   _Giving consecutive sentences a similar form._

Example from the text with line numbers: _____

_____

Effect: _____

- Persuasive technique: Definition:

_____   _Statements used by the author._

Example from the text with line numbers: _____

_____

Effect: _____

- Persuasive technique: Definition:

_____   _Evidence or research is given._

Example from the text with line numbers: _____

_____

Effect: _____

- Persuasive technique: Definition:

_____   _Words or phrases used several times in the text._

Example from the text with line numbers: _____

Effect: _____

3 EVALUATION

a) Research in Germany revealed that applicants with non-German names are less likely to be invited to an interview than candidates with a German-sounding name despite having the same qualifications. Therefore the scientists suggested introducing anonymous applications which convey information on the candidates' qualifications, but not on their ethnicity, age or gender. Write a comment in which you state your opinion on this proposal. Use at least three of the persuasive techniques from above. → S14.2

b) Write a letter to the editor commenting on Doreen Lawrence's article. State why you do/do not share her opinion on the need for more diversity in jobs. Think of more ways to support people from disadvantaged backgrounds. → S19.1

4 **TRUE OR FALSE** Tick the correct box. Give the line number(s) and the first and last three words of the quote from the text to prove your assertions.

	True	False
1. Doreen Lawrence is on her own in her fight for more diversity in top jobs. Line(s): _____		
2. If everybody has reason to believe in equal opportunity, the entire country will benefit. Line(s): _____		
3. The call for more diversity in top jobs is backed by research. Line(s): _____		
4. Ethnic minority groups ask for more support from the government. Line(s): _____		
5. Not having enough role models in their professions leads many people from ethnic minority groups to giving up on their ambitions in that field. Line(s): _____		
6. Once candidates from ethnic minority groups have successfully applied for a job, it is easier for them to progress. Line(s): _____		
7. Doreen Lawrence has doubts about whether progress with minorities being disadvantaged in their jobs is possible. Line(s): _____		
8. The Stephen Lawrence Charitable Trust plans to offer its services also to the private sector. Line(s): _____		

5 **MULTIPLE CHOICE** Which of the following statements sums up the text best? Tick the correct box.

☐ a) The lack of diversity in executive positions is a big issue in Britain. In order to tackle this problem, people from minority backgrounds ask for more support from the government.

☐ b) Britain is one of the very few countries worldwide which offers equal opportunities for everyone. Qualification and experience are the decisive factors for success, not ethnicity.

☐ c) In Britain, ethnic minority groups are clearly disadvantaged on the career ladder. They would rather be chosen for their own merits than through affirmative action, but support is still necessary.

A1 ◁)) **6 SHORT ANSWER** Listen to part 1 of an interview with Thomas Chatterton Williams about race, identity and power on the BBC Radio show *Hardtalk*. Give a short answer. You need not write complete sentences.

What was the situation like for Black people in the US when Thomas Chatterton Williams' father grew up?

_____

_____

7 MULTIPLE CHOICE Tick the correct answer.

1. Thomas Chatterton Williams' father taught him that …

☐ a) it is society that defines race. ☐ c) he needed to move like a Black man.

☐ b) race is biologically determined. ☐ d) outer appearance indicates one's ethnicity.

2. In 2012 Williams wrote an article in which he called for …

☐ a) Obama to promote Black identity. ☐ c) his children to celebrate their Black identity.

☐ b) more support for interracial couples. ☐ d) mixed-race Blacks emphasising their Black identity.

8 SHORT ANSWERS Give short answers. You need not write complete sentences.

1. What does the interviewer mean when he says that Chatterton's ideas have taken a U-turn?

_____

_____

2. Why does Chatterton consider it important that the French do not have the concept of the

one-drop rule? _____

_____

_____

one-drop rule The one-drop rule said that a child was considered Black when just one of its ancestors was Black.

A2 ◁)) **9 MULTIPLE CHOICE** Now listen to part 2. Tick the two correct options.

According to Williams, what needs to be done for us to be perceived as who we are is to …

☐ a) reinforce our sense of ourselves.

☐ b) reify the notion of Black and white.

☐ c) embrace racial categorisations.

☐ d) fight the racism that exists in the world.

☐ e) look ahead and past notions of Black and white.

10 SHORT ANSWER Give a short answer. You need not write complete sentences.

What does Williams mean when he calls for a childlike notion of race? _____

_____

11 MULTIPLE CHOICE

In order for multiethnic societies to work, Williams argues we need to …

☐ a) treat people as individuals. ☐ c) double down on efforts to integrate.

☐ b) change hierarchical arrangements. ☐ d) strive for a more homogenous society.

12 MEDIATION Last year, your family hosted a foreign exchange student from the US who you are still in touch with on a regular basis.
A few days ago, he told you that he is currently working on a project on 'othering' in his social science class and has asked you whether you have any material he could use. You sent him the following article, but he immediately replied telling you that all he understood was 'othering'.
Write an email back and explain to him what the article says about othering in general and about Jews in Germany in particular. → S19.4

> **TIP**
>
> Mark up relevant passages for your task (othering in general/of Jews, logic of inclusion/exclusion, critique of the cover).

Das Judentum und „die Deutschen"

In einer 1965 erschienenen Studie haben Norbert Elias und John L. Scotson aufgezeigt, dass bei dem Prozess der Ausgrenzung von Bevölkerungsgruppen eine Umwertung von Eigen-
5 schaften stattfindet: Eigenschaften, die bisher als zweitrangig galten – wie etwa die Religionszugehörigkeit –, werden von einer Mehrheit der Bevölkerung zu erstrangigen Eigenschaften erklärt. So wird ein grundlegender Unterschied
10 zwischen dem Eigenen und dem Anderen behauptet.

Aus einem Schuster, der gerne Schach spielt und übrigens auch Jude ist, wird plötzlich vor allem eines: ein Jude. Dieser Vorgang bedeutet,
15 dass das Othering wichtiger wird als das, was bisher als gemeinsame Grundlage der Gesellschaft wahrgenommen wurde: die als universal gesetzte Menschlichkeit. Und zugleich gelingt es der Mehrheit, sich im Akt des Aus-
20 schlusses ebenjene Menschlichkeit zuzusprechen und sich und ihren Eigenschaften universale Gültigkeit zu verleihen. Damit versichert sie sich einer einheitlichen Identität.

„Der Spiegel" hat kürzlich in seiner Reihe
25 „Geschichte" diesbezüglich ein umstrittenes Titelbild gewählt, als man mit dem Thema „Jüdisches Leben in Deutschland" den Deutschen eine „unbekannte Welt nebenan" eröffnen soll. Dazu werden zwei schäbig geklei-
30 dete Männer aufs Cover gesetzt, von denen sich einer frech mitten auf den Gehweg gesetzt hat.

[...] Hier wird das Judentum auf eine Weise dargestellt, die es als wesentlich vom „Deutschen" unterschieden kennzeichnet – ent-
35 weder aufgrund des äusserlichen Erscheinungsbildes oder aufgrund der Opferrolle, aufgrund von Riten, Sprache oder auch bestimmter Stigmata wie des übermässigen Reichtums oder der Heimatlosigkeit.
40 Das „Deutsche" erscheint immer als das genaue Gegenteil dessen, was als „jüdisch" definiert wurde, womit sich der Eindruck fest-

setzt, dass eine deutsche Mehrheitsgesellschaft ihre Identität sozusagen ex negativo, in Absetz-
45 ung zum „Anderen", bestimmt. Vor diesem Hintergrund ist die Wahl des Fotos der beiden orthodoxen, aus Osteuropa stammenden Juden auf dem Titelblatt der „Spiegel"-Ausgabe nur konsequent, aber umso skandalöser im Mecha-
50 nismus, der in dieser Wahl zum Ausdruck kommt.

Darin spiegelt sich eine Logik von Ein- und Ausschluss, die im Grunde allen in den vergangenen Jahrzehnten vorgeschlagenen Begriffs-
55 paaren gemeinsam ist, die dazu angetan sein sollten, das Verhältnis zwischen dem „Deutschen" und dem „Jüdischen" zu bestimmen wie etwa Insider/Outsider, Einheimischer/Fremder, Zentrum/Rand, Majorität/Minorität (und
60 deren „kleine" Literaturen). Gemein ist all diesen Begriffspaaren, dass sie den Primat des „Selbst" postulieren, d.h. die Vorstellung, das „Deutsche" sei das Universale, weil ursprünglich Gegebene, das „Jüdische" (das „Türkische" oder wie auch im-
65 mer) aber das Hinzugekommene, das als solches die Einheit der Nationalidentität stört oder bereichert.

Die Wertung ist in diesem Zusammenhang weniger von Bedeutung als die Tatsache, dass
70 mit diesen Begrifflichkeiten – wie gut gemeint sie auch sein mögen – ein binäres Denken unterstützt wird, das der Möglichkeit einer Integration des „Anderen" immer schon gegenläufig ist. Mehr noch: Diese Begrifflichkeiten schieben
75 dem „Anderen", dem „Juden", das Identitätsproblem unter, das im Grunde eines ist, das, wie wir gesehen haben, der modernen Gesellschaft als solcher eigen ist, der Mehrheit wie der Minderheit. Denn auch die Mehrheit braucht die „Anderen", von denen sie sich abgrenzen kann,
80 um ihre Identität zu bestimmen. Und die Minderheit hat ihre Identität unter Beweis zu stellen, da sie niemals ganz dazugehört.

Karin Neuburger, *Neue Zürcher Zeitung*, 2019

13 MONOLOGUE

a) Use the given pictures to talk about identity and migration.

b) Assess to what extent these pictures provide a comprehensive picture of identity and migration.

Partner A

14 MONOLOGUE

a) Use the given pictures to talk about migration and diversity.

b) Assess to what extent these pictures provide a comprehensive picture of migration and diversity.

Partner B

SUPPORT

1. Take brief notes on your graphic image and decide on the relevant aspects you want to talk about. You could start with your associations of the depicted shapes and how they relate to the topic.

2. The task "assess" asks you to express a well-founded opinion on the nature or quality of sb./sth. A well-founded opinion usually entails suitable examples to illustrate your arguments and back your opinion.

15 DIALOGUE You and your partner are given the chance to present a poster at the Haas Institute for a Fair and Inclusive Society on the challenges and opportunities migration poses for society. You have come across the given word cloud and want to use it as a starting point. Discuss and decide on how you want to address the issue and what additional impulses you would like to use. You can also integrate the pictures from your monologue tasks.

SUPPORT

Since this is a collaborative task, it is a good idea to make your process of developing the presentation transparent as well. Here are some phrases you might find useful in the process:

To get started:
Let's get started with … • The central issue/term is … • Who are we talking to?

To collect your ideas:
Why don't we … • What do you say, we … • Maybe we could …

To structure your ideas:
We need to structure our thoughts a bit. • It would be useful if we had some categories. •
We could put that down for … • That fits …

To focus (re-focus):
This seems to be our central point/aspect/argument. • I think we got off track a bit. •
Let's get back to …

To wrap up:
We need to/should come to an end. • I think this wraps it up nicely. • Yes, let's do it like that.

2 Choices in work and society

The Interestings

This extract is the beginning of a novel by American author Meg Wolitzer.
The scene takes place at a summer camp for young, artistic and creative people called "Spirit-in-the-Woods"
in the early 1970s.

On a warm night in early July of that long-evaporated year, the Interestings gathered for the very first time. They were only fifteen, sixteen, and they began to call themselves the
5 name with tentative irony. Julie Jacobson, an outsider and possibly even a freak, had been invited in for obscure reasons, and now she sat in a corner of the unswept floor and attempted to position herself so she would appear
10 unobtrusive yet not pathetic, which was a difficult balance. The teepee, designed ingeniously though built cheaply, was airless on nights like this one, when there was no wind to push in through the screen. Julie Jacobson
15 longed to unfold a leg or do the side-to-side motion with her jaw that sometimes set off a gratifying series of tiny percussive sounds inside her skull. But if she called attention to herself now, someone might start to wonder why she
20 was here; and really, she knew, she had no reason to be here at all. It had been miraculous when Ash Wolf had nodded to her earlier in the night at the row of sinks and asked if she wanted to come join her and some of the others later. Some
25 of the others. Even that wording was thrilling.

Julie had looked at her with a dumb, dripping face, which she then quickly dried with a thin towel from home. Jacobson, her mother had written along the puckered edge in red laundry
30 marker in a tentative hand that now seemed a little tragic. "Sure," she had said out of instinct. What if she'd said no? She liked to wonder afterward in a kind of strangely pleasurable, baroque horror. What if she'd turned down the
35 slightly flung invitation and went about her life, thudding obliviously along like a drunk person, a blind person, a moron, someone who thinks that the small packet of happiness she carries is enough. Yet having said "sure" at the sinks in the
40 girls' bathroom, here she was now, planted in the corner of an unfamiliar, ironic world. Irony was new to her and tasted oddly good, like a previously unavailable summer fruit. Soon, she

and the rest of them would be ironic much of the time, unable to answer an innocent question 45 without giving their words a snide little adjustment. Fairly soon after that, the snideness would soften, the irony would be mixed in with seriousness, and the years would shorten and fly. Then it wouldn't be long before they all found 50 themselves shocked and sad to be fully grown into their thicker, finalized adult selves, with almost no chance for reinvention.

That night, though, long before the shock and the sadness and the permanence, as they sat in 55 Boys' Teepee 3, their clothes bakery sweet from the very last washer-dryer loads at home, Ash Wolf said, "Every summer we sit here like this. We should call ourselves something." "Why?" said Goodman, her older brother. "So the world 60 can know just how unbelievably interesting we are?" "We could be called the Unbelievably Interesting Ones," said Ethan Figman. "How's that?" "The Interestings," said Ash. "That works."

So it was decided. "From this day forward, 65 because we are clearly the most interesting people who ever fucking lived," said Ethan, "because we are just so fucking compelling, our brains are swollen with intellectual thoughts, let us be known as the Interestings. And let 70 everyone who meets us falls down dead in our path from just how fucking interesting we are." In a ludicrously ceremonial moment they lifted paper cups and joints. Julie risked raising her cup of vodka and Tang – "V&T," they'd called it – 75 nodding gravely as she did this.

"Clink," Cathy Kiplinger said.

"Clink," said all the others.

The name was ironic, and the improvisational christening was jokily pretentious, but still, Julie 80 Jacobson thought, they were interesting. These teenagers around her, all of them from New York City, were like royalty and French movie stars, with a touch of something papal. Everyone at this camp was supposedly artistic, but here, as 85 far as she could tell, was the hot little nucleus of

the place. She had never met anyone like these people, they were interesting compared not only with the residents of Underhill, the New York
90 suburb where she'd lived since birth, but also compared with what was generally out there, which at the moment seemed baggy suited, nefarious, thoroughly repulsive.

From: Meg Wolitzer, *The Interestings*, 2013

5 tentative not certain • **10 unobtrusive** not attracting unnecessary attention • **10 pathetic** [pə'θetɪk] making you feel pity or sadness • **11 teepee** special type of (Indian) tent • **16 jaw** *Kiefer* • **17 gratifying** pleasing, giving satisfaction • **23 sink** *Waschbecken* • **25 wording** way sth is expressed in words • **26 dripping** very wet • **29 puckered** *gekräuselt* • **35 slightly flung** here: spoken without much care or thought • **36 to thud along** to walk with a heavy step • **36 oblivious** not aware of sth • **37 moron** *(infml)* idiot • **46 snide** *(infml)* criticising sb in an indirect way • **47 adjustment** correction • **68 compelling** very interesting and exciting • **73 ludicrous** ridiculous, absurd • **75 Tang** fruit-flavoured drink • **80 christening** *Taufe* • **80 pretentious** trying to appear important, intelligent, etc. • **84 papal** connected with the Pope • **92 baggy suited** wearing baggy *(ausgebeult)* trousers • **93 nefarious** criminal, immoral

→ To practise with closed reading comprehension tasks, go to tasks 4–7.

1 COMPREHENSION On a separate sheet of paper, describe who "The Interestings" are.

SUPPORT

1. From your memory, jot down key words on what you remember about "the Interestings".
2. Skim the excerpt and verify your key words. Add additional information (their ages, names, background, meeting place, motivation to become a group).
3. Before writing, structure your notes into categories. Number the categories as you want to present them. Begin with general information and move on to detailed aspects.

2 ANALYSIS Characterise Julie Jacobson by focussing on the image she has of herself and the point of view from which she is presented.

SUPPORT

1. Using a coloured marker, highlight the information about Julie, focusing on what she does (external action). With a different colour, mark the information about how she feels (internal action).
2. For each of the passages marked, come up with suitable adjectives to describe Julie. Then look at the passages you've marked again: underline phrases indicating how Julie sees herself.

Useful adjectives: communicative/quiet • self-confident/unsure of herself • spontaneous/ controlled • fearful/courageous • dominant/submissive • active/passive • bold/reserved • arrogant/modest • uninhibited/inhibited • extroverted/introverted

3. This novel is written from the third-person perspective. Still, it focusses on one character's view. Find passages illustrating this analysis and think about how this point of view influences the way we understand Julie's character.

3 EVALUATION "[I]t wouldn't be long before they all found themselves shocked and sad to be fully grown into their thicker, finalized adult selves, with almost no chance for reinvention." (ll.50–53 Comment on what this statement says about growing up.

SUPPORT

1. Circle the key words in the quote. Brainstorm each key word: What do you associate with the particular expression? Using your notes, rewrite the quote in your own words.
2. Decide on whether you agree or disagree with this view on growing up. Then find arguments to support your position. Come up with suitable examples to expand your arguments.
3. Order your arguments from least convincing to most convincing. Write your comment drawing from this outline (definition – opinion – arguments). In a final paragraph, sum up your opinion based on the arguments presented.

4 MULTIPLE CHOICE Tick the correct answers.

1. The excerpt describes how a group of young friends …

☐ a) are shaped by the creative summer camp they attend.

☐ b) come up with an idea on how to set themselves apart from others.

☐ c) decide to help a newcomer get to know the summer camp.

☐ d) look back to when they all met for the first time.

2. At the beginning of the scene, Julie Jacobson …

☐ a) doesn't want to draw unnecessary attention to herself.

☐ b) is sorry that she came to the teepee in the first place.

☐ c) wonders why her new friends call themselves interesting.

☐ d) realises the others invited her to play a joke on her.

3. When Julie was invited to the meeting by Ash, she …

☐ a) was unsure about how to answer.　　☐ c) was afraid about what the others might think.

☐ b) spontaneously agreed.　　☐ d) felt triumphant.

5 SENTENCE COMPLETION Complete the sentence.

Looking back, Julie believes that if she had declined the invitation, she would have _____

_____

6 TRUE OR FALSE Tick the correct box. Give the line number(s) and the first and last three words of the quote from the text to prove your assertions.

	True	False
1. Julie feels intrigued by the concept of irony. Line(s): _____		
2. The teenagers turn more ironic the older they get. Line(s): _____		
3. For them, growing older is full of possibilities. Line(s): _____		
4. The friends have repeatedly met at the summer camp. Line(s): _____		
5. The teenagers truly think they are extremely interesting. Line(s): _____		

7 SHORT ANSWERS Give three reasons why Julie Jacobson is fascinated by "The Interestings".

_____

_____

TIP

Read through the tasks carefully before listening. Using a pencil, circle the key words in the tasks. It will help you to listen for the information you need to complete the tasks. Listen to the recording twice.

A1 ◁)) **8** TABLE COMPLETION Listen to an interview with 16-year-old Deanna Lane, who is a NEET – a young person **n**ot in **e**ducation, **e**mployment or **t**raining. Complete the table with information from the interview.

1. Deanna is uncertain about:	
2. If she were able to choose freely, she would:	
3. Reasons why Deanna cannot go to college:	

FACT FILE

The EMA (Education Maintenance Allowance) provided financial support to young people from low income families, but was abolished in England in 2012. The GCSE (General Certificate of Education) is a set of exams taken at the age of 16 in the UK and it roughly corresponds to the German *Realschulabschluss*. Students must take at least four subjects. Most take about seven.

9 MATCHING Match the correct sentence beginnings and endings. There are two extra endings.

1 Deanna criticises the lack of guidance available		A who has not found something to do.
		B after graduation isn't a problem.
2 Many youths think that getting a job		C who is not continuing her education.
		D after leaving school.
3 Of her friends, Deanna is the only one		E while she was still in school.

10 MULTIPLE CHOICE Tick the correct box to complete the following sentences. Only one answer is correct.

1. Deanna's first job interview …

☐ a) turned out just as she expected.   ☐ c) scared her from start to finish.

☐ b) was very easy to manage.   ☐ d) left her with a positive feeling.

2. Overall, Deanna has been …

☐ a) putting a lot of effort into finding a job.   ☐ c) advised poorly by the local job centre.

☐ b) unsure about how to find a job.   ☐ d) in touch with many employers.

11 SHORT ANSWERS Give a short answer using key words.

1. Why is Deanna's young age a problem? _____

_____

2. Why is it difficult for Deanna's parents to support their daughter? _____

_____

3. What is the most important reason for Deanna to find a job? _____

_____

12 MEDIATION Together with its American partner school, your school has decided to create an online magazine focussing on how the Corona pandemic has affected young people's daily lives around the globe. It is your task to write an article about how German graduates' plans for their gap years have been disrupted. Draw your information from the following two testimonies you have found in the German news magazine *Der Spiegel*.

„So hatte ich mir das Ganze nicht vorgestellt"

„Ich habe mein Abi 2019 gemacht und wollte nicht direkt danach mit dem Studium beginnen. Für mich stand fest, dass ich erst einmal zurück nach Vancouver gehe, wo ich in der neunten
5 Klasse schon für ein Auslandsjahr gewesen war. Im Juli 2019 brach ich also nach Kanada auf. Ich wollte ein Jahr lang arbeiten und herumreisen, ‚Work and Travel' eben. Anfangs übernahm ich kleinere Jobs, beispielsweise im Fundraising.
10 Nach eineinhalb Monaten bekam ich ein traumhaftes Angebot: ein Job als Fotograf in Banff. Ich blieb sechs Monate dort, arbeitete und wanderte.

Danach hatte ich den Drang, Kanada noch
15 weiter zu erkunden, und kündigte. Im Nachhinein war das ein Fehler, weil ich mit dem Job auch während Corona in Kanada hätte bleiben können - dann hätte ich genug Geld verdient. So aber musste ich wegen der Pandemie alle meine
20 Pläne ändern und nach Deutschland zurück. Das Auswärtige Amt hatte zur Rückreise aufgerufen, und außerdem war ich pleite. Die Tage bis zu meinem Rückflug verbrachte ich in Hostels, völlig perplex und teilweise sehr einsam.
25 Ende März kam ich dann in München an – verfrüht, und ohne jeglichen Plan was ich bis zum Studienbeginn machen sollte. Die folgenden Monate zu Hause bei meinen Eltern verbrachte ich mit Kochen, Skypen und Däumchen
30 drehen, die Zeit hat sich wirklich gezogen. Es fühlt sich so an, als hätte man mir einen Teil dieser wertvollen Lebenserfahrung weggenommen. Ich hatte mich so auf die anstehenden Reisen gefreut, ich war schließlich in Kanada, um
35 neue Ecken der Erde zu entdecken und unterschiedliche Jobs auszuprobieren. Ich finde es super wichtig, als junger Mensch die Erfahrung zu machen, allein zu verreisen."

(Kenzo, 20 Jahre, aus München)

40 „Nach meinem Abi im Juni dieses Jahres wollte ich eigentlich zu meiner Gastfamilie nach Ohio fliegen, bei der ich während der Schulzeit ein Jahr gelebt hatte, und dann eine kleine Rundrei-
se durch die USA machen. Danach hatte ich ge-
45 plant, Freunde in Luxemburg und Spanien zu besuchen, schließlich hätte ich endlich Zeit dafür gehabt. Meine Reise musste ich wegen Corona aber komplett abblasen. Ich war richtig traurig, weil ich meine Gastfamilie sehr ver-
50 misse, wir haben uns lange nicht gesehen.

Im Herbst wollte ich eigentlich in Hamburg mein Management-Studium beginnen. Das kam für mich aber in diesen unsicheren Zeiten auch nicht mehr infrage. Ich wollte kein Versuchska-
55 ninchen sein, während das Hochschulsystem sich der neuen Situation anpasst. So habe ich mir das Studieren einfach nicht vorgestellt. Deshalb habe ich mich entschieden, doch nicht im Herbst mit dem Studium zu beginnen, son-
60 dern zu warten. Meine Eltern fanden das nicht gerade toll, hatten aber auch Verständnis für meine Entscheidung.

Ich arbeite schon seit Januar letzten Jahres nebenbei in der Elbphilharmonie, wo ich bei Konzerten an der Garderobe oder am Eingang
65 eingesetzt werde. Weder mir noch meiner Familie erschien der Minijob aber ausreichend als Überbrückung für meine abgesagten Reise- und Studienpläne. ‚Du kannst ja nicht ein Jahr zu Hause rumchillen!', sagte mein Freund. Also
70 musste ich mir einen neuen Plan überlegen.

Um das Beste aus diesem Jahr herauszuholen, absolviere ich nun ein FSJ an einer Hamburger Grundschule. Hier unterstütze und beschäftige ich zwei Kinder mit geistiger Entwicklungs-
75 störung. Das ist anstrengend, aber es macht mir Spaß. Vielleicht krempele ich meine Studienpläne jetzt noch mal völlig um und studiere ab Herbst 2021 Lehramt.

Im Endeffekt bin ich froh darüber, dass ich
80 jetzt dieses FSJ mache. Ich war mir nicht hundertprozentig sicher, was ich studieren will – nun habe ich ein paar Monate Zeit, mir das zu überlegen, Erfahrungen zu sammeln. Und ich weiß jetzt, wie es ist, acht Stunden am Tag zu ar-
85 beiten und selbstständiger zu sein."

(Yari, 19 Jahre, aus Hamburg)

Laura Naima Kabelka, *Der Spiegel*, 2020

SUPPORT

1. Take a closer look at the mediation task and complete the missing information.

   • context: _____

   _____

   • addressee: _____

   • target text: _____

   • register/style: _____

   • purpose/your focus: _____

   _____

2. For each of the two graduates interviewed, select the information which is relevant to the task. Use different colours to mark up passages regarding the following categories:
   • reasons for taking a gap year
   • original plans
   • new plans
   • if and how the pandemic has changed their outlook/perspective

3. Go through the passages you marked and decide whether they contain words that cannot be translated literally (e.g. *Däumchen drehen*) or require additional information for readers unfamiliar with the German system of education (e.g. *Abitur*). Paraphrase these expressions.

4. Create a chart with the categories from task 2 and fill in the information you marked up in English.

Reasons for taking a gap year	Original plans	New plans	If and how the pandemic has changed their outlook/perspective
Didn't want to study immediately after graduation ...			

5. Using your notes from task 4, write your article. Remember to begin with a catchy phrase to grab your readers' attention. You can round your text off by giving your own opinion. Don't forget to come up with a suitable headline.

FACT FILE

Bei einem Freiwilligen Sozialen Jahr (FSJ) arbeiten junge Menschen für eine Dauer von 6 bis 18 Monaten in einer sozialen Einrichtung mit.
Voraussetzung für eine Bewerbung für ein FSJ ist ein Schulabschluss und ein Höchstalter von 26 Jahren.
Man erhält dafür kein Gehalt, in der Regel jedoch ein Taschengeld oder einen Zuschuss zu Unterkunft und Verpflegung und hat einen Urlaubsanspruch.

13 MONOLOGUE You and a partner are invited to give a speech at a youth conference titled "Can young people change the world for the better"? Both of you are looking for different aspects to focus on and the appropriate media to use.

Partner A

Give a five-minute talk intended to convince your partner of the positive impact of youth volunteering.
- Explain the impact of volunteering by providing examples.
- Use the prompts provided (photo and text) as a starting point, explaining whether you would consider using them in your speech.
- Take possible objections into account.

'Doing good' is a volunteer's most likely motivation

The top three motivations listed in order are:
- I wanted to improve things/help people (46 %)
- The cause was important to me (31 %)
- I had spare time to do it (25 %)

Whereas the least common motivations for volunteering were:
- I felt there was no-one else to do it (7 %)
- It helps me get on in my career (7 %)
- It gives me a chance to get a recognised qualification (2 %)

Statistics from the Third Sector Project website, 2018

Partner B

Give a five-minute talk intended to convince your partner of the positive impact of youth environmental activism.
- Explain the impact of youth environmental activism by providing examples.
- Use the prompts provided (photo and text) as a starting point, explaining whether you would consider using them in your speech.
- Take possible objections into account.

Environment and climate change

- In Africa, Asia, and Latin America, where more than 1 billion young men and women live, climate change will continue to affect all aspects of food security.
- Some 84% of surveyed young people agree that they need more information to prevent climate change.
- About 73% of surveyed youth say they currently feel the effects of climate change.
- Some 89% of youth respondents say young people can make a difference on climate change.

Statistics from the UN Secretary-General's Youth Envoy report, 2015

14 **DIALOGUE** Together with your partner, agree on three aspects you want to include in your final speech.
   a) Discuss the ideas from your presentation task as well the additional aspects (the photos and the quote) presented below. Choose the most convincing ones.
   b) Agree on how to deal with sceptics who doubt young people truly have the power to achieve change.
   c) Discuss the advantages and disadvantages of different media to reach out to (young) people.
   You have ten minutes.

Use online platforms to reach others

There's never been a greater time in history for reaching out to millions of people around the world. You've probably seen how a single Twitter hashtag can create massive social awareness. What hashtags can you contribute to, or even create?

If longer writing is more your thing, writing for an online portal [...] is a great place to start. You can write blogs and original content [...] to reach new audiences, and if it's featured then you could see your article reaching thousands of people.

From ONE Youth Ambassador
Danee McGuire's blog post
"6 things young people can do to change the world",
on the One website, 2017

USEFUL PHRASES

Stating your case:
Let me begin by …
In my opinion, …
I am convinced that …
I would like to make several/three/… points.
First of all … / Secondly, … / Thirdly, …
It is also important to understand that …
My point is that …
For this reason …

Interacting with others:
How do you feel about this?
I'm not sure it's as simple as that.
That's a good idea.
That sounds very convincing to me.
I totally agree with you.
I can (absolutely) go along with that.
I'm sure we both agree on …
What has become clear in our discussion is that …

3 The media

We need to rethink social media before it's too late. We've accepted a Faustian bargain

A business model that alters the way we think, act, and live our lives has us heading toward dystopia

When people envision technology overtaking society, many think of The Terminator and bulletproof robots. Or Big Brother in George Orwell's *Nineteen Eighty-Four*, a symbol of
5 external, omnipotent oppression.

But in all likelihood, dystopian technology will not strong-arm us. Instead, we'll unwittingly submit ourselves to a devil's bargain: freely trade our subconscious preferences for memes, our
10 social cohesion for instant connection, and the truth for what we want to hear.

Indeed, as former insiders at Google, Twitter, Facebook, Instagram and YouTube attest in our new documentary, *The Social Dilemma*, this is
15 already happening. We already live in a version of Aldous Huxley's *Brave New World*. As Neil Postman puts it in his 1985 book *Amusing Ourselves to Death: Public Discourse in the Age of Show Business*:
20 "In Huxley's vision, no Big Brother is required to deprive people of their autonomy, maturity, and history. As he saw it, people will come to love their oppression, to adore the technologies that undo their capacities to think".
25 The technology that threatens our society, democracy, and mental health is lurking in our bedrooms, sometimes lying on our pillows, as we fall asleep. We awake to its call, bring its chiming notifications to dinner, and blindly trust where it
30 guides us. We scroll insatiably, unsuspecting that the technology that connects us, especially now in a distanced world, is also controlling us.

Our social media platforms are powered by a surveillance-based business model designed to
35 mine, manipulate, and extract our human experiences at any cost, causing a breakdown of our information ecosystem and shared sense of truth worldwide. This extractive business model is not built for us but built to exploit us.
40 A third of American adults, and nearly half of those aged 18–29, say they are online "almost constantly". But, unlike the citizens of *Brave New World*, we're miserable. As our time online has gone up, so have anxiety, depression and suicide
45 rates, particularly among youth.

Social media is also derailing productive public discourse. A largely ignored internal memo to senior executives at Facebook in 2018 explained: "Our algorithms exploit the human brain's attraction to divisiveness." Left
50 unchecked, the algorithms will feed users "more and more divisive content in an effort to gain user attention and increase time on the platform".

In 2014, Pew Research Center found that
55 partisan antipathy and division in America is "deeper and more extensive than at any point in the last two decades". Over the past six years, social media has only exacerbated these sentiments. In 2019, 77 % of Republicans and
60 72 % of Democrats said voters in both parties "not only disagree over plans and policies, but also cannot agree on the basic facts".

In *The Social Dilemma*, Tristan Harris, a former Google design ethicist and the co-
65 founder of the Center for Humane Technology, points out that far before technology overpowers human strengths, it will overwhelm human weaknesses. Sophisticated algorithms learn our emotional vulnerabilities and exploit them for
70 profit in insidious ways.

By surveilling nearly all of our online activity, social media platforms can now predict our emotions and behaviors. They leverage these insights and auction us to the highest
75 advertising bidder, and they have consequently become some of the richest companies in the history of the world.

But users aren't just being sold a pair of shoes. The targeting capabilities of these platforms
80 give anyone with a motive the power and precision to influence us cheaply and with phenomenal ease. Disinformation campaigns have been cited in more than 70 countries, and doubled from 2017 to 2019.
85 The whistleblower Sophie Zhang has revealed how pervasive the problem is on Facebook's platform, and how little the company acts on it. Facebook recently rolled out a series of updates to mitigate political misinformation in the
90

upcoming US presidential election, including a bar on political ads one week before election day, but these measures are too little, too late, and they do not address the fundamental problem of
95 their exploitative business model.

After nearly three years of working on this film, I now see "the social dilemma" as a foundational problem of our time, underlying many of the other societal conflicts that require
100 compromise and a shared understanding to fix. If two sides are constantly fed reflections of their pre-existing ideologies and outrageous straw men of opposing views, we will never be able to build bridges and heal the challenges that
105 plague humanity.

But there is hope. In *The Terminator* sequels, Arnold Schwarzenegger comes back as a good guy. "Who sent you?" John Connor asks. The Terminator answers, "You did. Thirty-five years from now, you reprogrammed me to be your
110 protector."

In the absence of time travel, the solution needs to incorporate the work and voices of devoted activists, organizations, scholars, and those who have experienced the harms of
115 exploitative technology, which amplifies systemic oppression and inequality. We can't rely on the people who created the problem to be the ones to solve it. And I won't trust these social media companies until they change their
120 business model to serve us, the public. Humans created this technology, and we can – and have a responsibility to – change it.

Jeff Orlowski, *The Guardian*, 2020

---

2 The Terminator a part-machine, part-human character in a famous science fiction film • **3 Big Brother** a character on posters and telescreens in George Orwell's novel who represents the leadership of the state • **9 meme** an idea or behaviour that spreads from person to person • **16 Brave New World** a novel whose setting is a state with complete control over people's lives • **71 insidious** something insidious is harmful and develops slowly so that people don't notice it until it is too late • **74 to leverage** to make use of **90 to mitigate** to make less harmful • **102 straw men** weak arguments that can easily be disproved

→ To practise with closed reading comprehension tasks, go to task 4.

1 COMPREHENSION Summarise the writer's ideas on the effects of social media use and on possible solutions to the problem.

SUPPORT

1. Make a note of key ideas in the text. Remember to concentrate on the topic in the task. Add information that is important and remove ideas that are not about effects or solutions.
2. Sort your ideas into two sections (effects and solutions).
3. Make a note of a central idea in the text for your introduction and an idea representing the message of the text for the conclusion.

2 ANALYSIS
a) Explain why the text can be divided into three sections.
b) Examine the writer's choice of words in the opening paragraphs (up to "controlling us", l. 32).

SUPPORT

1. For task 2 a): Identify three sections and write down a phrase or heading for each of them.

   Line(s): _____

   Line(s): _____

   Line(s): _____

2. For task 2 b): Using a marker, highlight words in the text that are associated with evil and adjectives or adverbs referring to the users' behaviour.
3. For task 2 b): Note down a phrase or sentence for each idea to explain the purpose of the words you have highlighted.

3 **EVALUATION** Write a letter to the editor of the newspaper responding to the article. Include your views on the writer's criticisms, other aspects of social media and possible solutions. → S19.1

SUPPORT

1. You are going to discuss the topic and reach an informed conclusion at the end.
   When you are asked to discuss the arguments in the text and express an opinion on them, remember that you must attract and retain the attention of readers. You will need
   • a clear statement at the beginning, which can take the form of a question for readers to think about
   • ideas agreeing or disagreeing with the text's arguments
   • a concluding statement that emphasises your opinion

   Start with ideas for the main section, which can include:
   • the role of social media users
   • social media: benefits and problems
   • solutions

   Now write down an idea for your opening statement and your conclusion.
   Reread your notes. They should be sorted logically and should not repeat points already made.

2. Letter writing:
   In this context you will not normally be expected to begin with an address and date, but you can do.
   Your letter should begin as follows:
   • Re: "[headline and date of article]"
   • "To the Editor" or "Sir/Madam"

   The main body should consist of several paragraphs, each dealing with a distinct aspect of your text.
   End with your name and the town you live in.

USEFUL PHRASES

With reference to your article of [26 September 2021], "[Dog bites men in park]" …
In his/her article dated/from …, the author stated that …
After carefully studying the article, I am sorry to say that/would like to express doubts about/to add that …
I definitely support/agree with the author's opinion on …
I am very glad that this topic has finally been …
It should be remembered that …
The idea/suggestion that …
The writer makes no mention of …
The writer fails to appreciate …
I was hoping for a more impartial treatment of/would appreciate more objectivity when …
In my experience …
An option the author did not consider would be to …
Undoubtedly, it would be more acceptable if …

4 **TRUE OR FALSE** Tick the correct box. Give the line number(s) and the first and last three words of the quote from the text to prove your assertions.

According to the writer:	True	False
1. We don't realise that we accept the influence of social media technology. Line(s): _____		
2. We generally escape from the influence of social media at night. Line(s): _____		
3. Social media gives us an accurate picture of the world around us. Line(s): _____		
4. Mental health problems have got worse thanks to social media. Line(s): _____		
5. Social media has helped to reduce political disagreements. Line(s): _____		
6. Social media companies sell information on users for as much money as possible. Line(s): _____		
7. The way companies use information is simply a commercial transaction. Line(s): _____		
8. Inaccurate information is a widespread problem on one popular social media site. Line(s): _____		
9. Facebook's action before the presidential election was very effective. Line(s): _____		
10. We can expect the social media companies to find an answer to 'the social dilemma'. Line(s): _____		

TIP

Exam practice
Try doing these tasks in strict exam conditions, for example using these rules:
• You will hear the recording twice. You have **2 minutes** to look at the task.
• You will have **1 minute** to finalise your answers after the second listening.

A1 ◁)) **5** MULTIPLE CHOICE Listen to a report on conspiracy theories broadcast a few weeks after Joe Biden became US president. Choose the best answer a), b) or c).

1. Following the presidential election, a majority of Americans …

☐ a) expected Donald Trump to be the new president.

☐ b) felt that the election had been fair.

☐ c) thought that the election had been decided by cheating.

2. In an interview, Bonnie Garland says that …

☐ a) all American presidents have been born in the US.

☐ b) coronavirus is a very dangerous disease.

☐ c) American astronauts didn't land on the moon.

3. Research suggests that a minority of Americans believe that …

☐ a) President Obama really was born in the US.

☐ b) recent shooting incidents were performed by actors.

☐ c) the attacks on September 11, 2001 were the work of foreign terrorists.

4. Believers in conspiracies about President Kennedy tried to find people who agreed with them by …

☐ a) making a movie. ☐ b) meeting at libraries. ☐ c) writing to newspapers.

5. People who spread disinformation …

☐ a) aim to influence public beliefs about politics.

☐ b) are not motivated by financial gain.

☐ c) want to give the public accurate news.

6 SHORT ANSWERS Answer the questions in 1 to 8 words.

1. Who did President Trump blame for not acting against fraud at the election?

_____

2. What proportion of Americans believed that fraud influenced the election result?

_____

3. How were voting machines said to have falsified the election result?

_____

4. When people take action on the basis of false information, there is a threat to communities and to which other people?

_____

5. What has been done for security in Washington, DC?

_____

6. The spread of conspiracy theories has changed people's thinking. What action do they now believe is acceptable?

_____

7. Why might things get better after the pandemic?

_____

7 MEDIATION You are in a team of researchers in a project on "The Media in the 21st Century". You are to write an article on the work of journalists and have chosen the report below as your source of information. Write your article on how the freedom of the press has been impaired, based on the ideas in the text.

Neue Dimension der Gewalt gegen Medienschaffende in Deutschland

Auf der aktuellen Rangliste der Pressefreiheit landet Deutschland nicht mehr in der Kategorie „gut" und rutscht von Rang 11 auf Rang 13 ab. Die Organisation Reporter ohne Grenzen, die die
5 jährliche Rangliste veröffentlicht, bezeichnet die Lage nun nur noch als „zufriedenstellend". Der Grund: eine „noch nie dagewesene Dimension" der Gewalt gegen Medienschaffende.

Die Organisation zählte in Deutschland 65
10 gewalttätige Angriffe gegen Journalist:innen – die Zahl hat sich damit im Vergleich zum Vorjahr verfünffacht. Viele der Übergriffe fanden Reporter ohne Grenzen zufolge auf oder am Rande von Demonstrationen gegen die Corona-Maßnah-
15 men statt. Vorstandssprecher des Vereins Michael Rediske nennt das „ein deutliches Alarmsignal".

Doch auch weltweit beobachtet Reporter ohne Grenzen Auswirkungen der Pandemie auf
20 die Pressefreiheit. Insbesondere die Regierungen und Regimes repressiver Staaten missbrauchten die Pandemie als Vorwand, um die Pressefreiheit weiter einzuschränken. Als Beispiel nennt Reporter ohne Grenzen Ägypten
25 (Rang 166), wo die Veröffentlichung aller nicht-offiziellen Infektionszahlen verboten wurde. In Syrien (Rang 173) verhängte das Regime eine Nachrichtensperre für alle Medien außer der staatlichen Nachrichtenagentur.
30 Die Präsidenten Donald Trump in den USA (Rang 44) und Jair Bolsonaro in Brasilien (Rang 111) verbreiteten Falschaussagen über Covid-19 und hetzten gegen Journalist:innen. Damit schufen sie ein „Klima der Aggressivität
35 und des Misstrauens", heißt es in dem Bericht von Reporter ohne Grenzen. Dies bestätigte die Journalistin Patrícia Campos Mello in einer Pressekonferenz von Reporter ohne Grenzen. Gegen Fake News auf Facebook sei durch kor-
40 rekte journalistische Informationen kaum anzukommen – das erlebe sie gerade an einer Desinformationskampagne gegen sie persönlich, die auch Präsident Bolsonaro unterstütze.

Auch der US-amerikanische Politikwissen-
45 schaftler Francis Fukuyama sieht die Macht der großen Internetkonzerne Twitter, Google und Facebook als Bedrohung für die Pressefreiheit.

„Der Großteil unserer Kommunikation basiert mittlerweile auf zumindest einer dieser Plattformen", so Fukuyama in der
50 Pressekonferenz. „Es gibt Länder, dort ist Facebook der einzige Weg, über den Menschen gerade noch miteinander reden." Doch die Geschäftsmodelle der Plattformen befeuerten die Verbreitung von Fake News und
55 Verschwörungstheorien.

Ganz unabhängig von der Pandemie beobachtete Reporter ohne Grenzen neue problematische Entwicklungen der Pressefreiheit – auch in Europa. In Ungarn (Rang 92) schaltete
60 die Regierung „zwei unabhängige wichtige Medien defacto aus". Im Zusammenhang mit der Berichterstattung über Migration seien mehrere Reporter:innen in Griechenland (Rang 70) festgenommen worden. In Belarus (Rang 158) kam
65 es im Laufe des Jahres 2020 zu vorübergehenden Festnahmen von mehr als 400 Medienschaffenden, die über Massenproteste nach der umstrittenen Präsidentenwahl berichtet hatten.

Die belarussische Oppositionsführerin Swjat-
70 lana Zichanouskaja, die mittlerweile in Litauen im Exil lebt, äußerte sich auf der Pressekonferenz von Reporter ohne Grenzen zu den Zuständen für Journalist:innen in ihrem Land. „Sie werden geschlagen, ihr Equipment wird zer-
75 stört, sie werden massiv verfolgt und ihnen wird der Zugang zu Informationen verweigert." Auch ihr Ehemann, der Blogger Sjarhej Zichanouski, sitzt mittlerweile seit 11 Monaten im Gefängnis. „Sein ‚Fehler' war, dass er den Mut fand, die
80 Wahrheit zu zeigen."

Die meisten Journalist:innen sind laut Reporter ohne Grenzen aktuell in China inhaftiert. Das Land stellt damit eines der Schlusslichter auf der Liste der 180 Länder dar. Dahinter liegen
85 noch Turkmenistan, Nordkorea und Eritrea.

Doch es gibt auch in einigen Regionen Grund zum Aufatmen: In einigen Subsahara-Ländern wie Burundi oder Mali verbesserte sich die Situation für Medienschaffende und in den nord-
90 europäischen Ländern Norwegen, Finnland und Schweden (Rang 1 bis 3) konnte sich ein hoher Grad an Pressefreiheit auch in der Pandemiezeit weiter durchsetzen.

Pia Stenner, Netzpolitik website, 2021

8 MONOLOGUE Describe a cartoon and explain its message.

Partner A

So I looked at your Facebook page ... oh man ... there's no way you're getting this job!

Partner B

"I'm trying to see if there's any truth to the rumor I started."

TIP

- If you are preparing for a speaking task with preparation time, make notes.
- Give yourself 5 minutes to jot down the words you need for important elements in the picture, then make notes on the idea behind the cartoon.
- If possible, include an example from your own or other people's experiences.

- When the 5 minutes are up, reset your timer, then speak about the cartoon. Make an effort to avoid speaking quickly: imagine you are speaking to a large audience. Use all of your time so that there is no 'embarrassing silence' before the 5 minutes are up.

9 DIALOGUE Selfies are an integral part of modern life. People take selfies to show that they want to ...

| be the centre of attention | remember special moments | show where they are and what they are doing |

With a partner, discuss which situations people want to look important in.

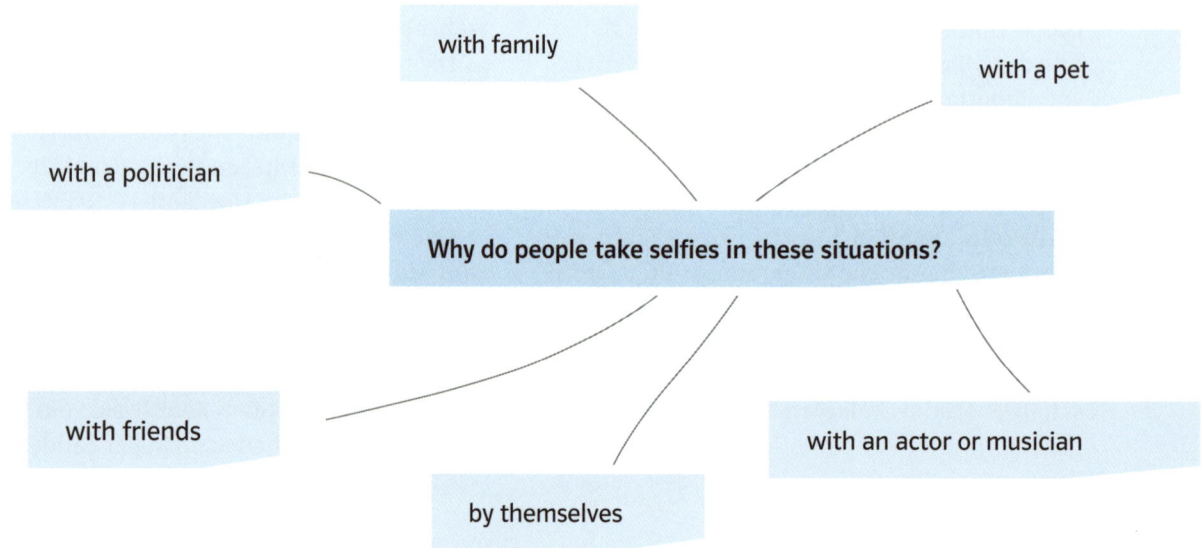

with family

with a pet

with a politician

Why do people take selfies in these situations?

with friends

with an actor or musician

by themselves

TIP

There is no preparation time for this task. If you are on your own, take a few seconds to look at the ideas, then try to speak about each of them for 3 minutes.

If you have a partner, talk about all of the ideas with them. Your discussion should last for 5 minutes.

Make sure that you interact with your partner and use some of the following useful phrases.

USEFUL PHRASES

Agreeing with your partner:
- Oh, definitely!
- Yes, I'm sure that's right/… that's a good idea.
- Yes, I'd go along with that.

Disagreeing/reacting to your partner (sceptically):
- But don't you think (that … is more important)?
- Well, that's not how I see it.

Bringing in your partner:
- What about …? How do you see that?
- I think that's a good idea don't you [name]?

Explaining or correcting yourself:
- It seems to me that …
- My idea is that …

Concluding negotiations:
- We seem to agree that … is the best idea.
- Well, we'll have to agree/to disagree (on that one)!

When you're stuck:
- Oh! I've forgotten what I was going to say!
- (What's the word?) It's on the tip of my tongue.

10 DIALOGUE Role play: Nowadays people get their news from different sources: social media sites, television and radio, newspapers and magazines. Take on one of the roles (A or B) in a discussion of the advantages and disadvantages of traditional news sources (TV, radio, newspapers) and news from social media sources.

- Student A argues the case for traditional media.
- Student B argues the case for social media.

TIP

Consider these ideas in your arguments:
- accuracy of news reports
- the audience that can be reached
- the time it takes to report
- users' reactions to reports
- the ability to react to new developments

4 Tradition and change in the UK

The United Kingdom is too precious to be lost to narrow nationalism

Nations and regions must join forces to ensure a healthy future for the union.

If the United Kingdom is to survive, it will have to change fundamentally, so that Scotland does not secede and our regions can once again feel part of it.

5   The shift in votes that gave the Conservatives an 80-seat majority does not signal a country at ease with itself or settling down to a post-Brexit stability. Nor does it herald a newfound unity or even an emerging national consensus.

10   Recent events are better understood as resulting from the power of competing nationalisms: Brexit nationalism, seeking national independence from Europe; Scottish nationalism; Welsh nationalism; and Irish and 15 Ulster nationalisms. The risk is that "getting Brexit done" is leaving Britain undone and, by destabilising the careful balance between the Irish and British identities in Northern Ireland, threatening the very existence of the United 20 Kingdom.

    While each nationalism considers itself unique and incontrovertibly powerful, their rise owes far more to common problems shared in every part of the UK: anxieties about stagnating 25 incomes, the rundown of manufacturing, insecure employment, poor-quality public services, boarded-up high streets, a lethal cocktail when combined with a strong sense of cultural loss and of a globalisation that seems 30 akin to a train that has run out of control. [...]

    In this respect, last month's election result seems less like an enthusiastic endorsement of any party than a plea for radical change. The old postwar social contract, based on times when 35 manufacturing, making a product in which you had pride, and mining which kept the nation's lights on, gave people dignity and respect, is seen as at breaking point, with each of its four pillars approaching collapse.

    First, for millions, work no longer pays. 40 Second, no matter how hard many strive, opportunities for upward mobility seem limited. Parents no longer feel confident that the next generation will do as well as the last. Third, with boardroom excesses, a bankers' bonus culture 45 and shocking inequalities in income, top people's pay can never again be justified as the result of merit and hard work. Finally, our 75-year-old safety net looks threadbare when in every town and city child poverty and 50 homelessness are rising and food banks, clothing banks, bedding banks, baby banks and other charities are substituting for a welfare state in retreat. All of this is magnified by the growing income and wealth gap between 55 London and the north that is far more extreme than in almost every European nation and the US's richer and poorer states. There is an ever-widening divide in how people perceive their future: how, the further you are from the centre 60 of power, the more you feel undervalued and unfairly treated. Only as NHS patients do people feel treated as equals, though there are increasing regional and social class disparities. [...] 65

    Nationalism can exploit these injustices but it cannot end them. While the Conservatives are the current beneficiaries of the revolt of the regions, their promise of a northern renaissance will have to mean more than love-bombing the 70 regions with a few infrastructure projects and an airline rescue. Instead, we must deliver a radical alternative to nationalism. It must start with a plan to address economic insecurity. But it must

75 also recognise that, in a multinational state that is asymmetric (83 % of its voters lie in one nation) and where financial, political and administrative power is concentrated in just one city far to the south, the outlying nations and 80 regions require new powers of initiative as decision-making centres – which, given our history as a unitary state, would be something akin to a British constitutional revolution. [...]

When George Orwell made the distinction 85 between patriots who love their country and nationalists who see life as a constant struggle between an "us" and a "them" and invent enemies – and grievances – where none exist, he called for a "moral effort" to defeat nationalist ideologies. 90

In 2020, that means rediscovering the value of empathy and solidarity between nations and regions and the benefits that can flow from cooperation and sharing in pursuit of great causes: from jointly tackling climate change to 95 offering the same floor of rights to universal health, social care and welfare services in every part of the UK.

Only then will we start to prove that the United Kingdom is united by more than its 100 name.

Gordon Brown (Prime Minister from 2007 to 2010),
The Guardian, 2020

---

precious of great value • **3 to secede** to leave officially, leave an organisation of states • **5 shift in votes that gave the Conservatives an 80-seat majority** *here: Refers to the General Election, November 2019, in which the Tories won a clear majority in the House of Commons* • **8 to herald sth** to be a sign that sth is going to happen • **22 incontrovertibly** without question because it is true • **30 to be akin to sth** to be similar to/like sth • **31 last month's election** *here:* General Election, November 2019 • **49 threadbare** worn, *here:* no longer good enough • **52 baby bank** a charity providing second-hand clothes and equipment to help parents with the costs of having a baby/child • **68 beneficiary** sb who has an advantage/profits from sth • **72 airline rescue** a reference to the government bailout of the tour operator Thomas Cook in 2019 • **89 moral effort** *here:* an attempt by people to stand up for what is right

→ To practise with closed reading comprehension tasks, go to tasks 4–6.

1 COMPREHENSION

a) Outline the reasons given in the text why the 2019 General Election result was not an expression of support for any particular party.

b) Suggest where the photos in the text might be used to illustrate a point made by the author and explain the reasons for your choice.

TIP

Scan the text for any references to the election and its result. This will help you find appropriate passages in the text.
Understanding the meaning of the word 'endorsement' will help you too.

SUPPORT

In your own words, say what is meant by the following quotes from the text:

1. "a country at ease with itself" (ll. 6–7)

_____

_____

2. "'getting Brexit done' is leaving Britain undone" (ll. 15–16)

_____

_____

3. "The Conservatives are the current beneficiaries" (ll. 67–68)

_____

_____

4. "love-bombing" (l. 70)

_____

_____

2 ANALYSIS Analyse the author's line of argument and how he tries to convince the reader of his point of view. Use text evidence to support your answer.

SUPPORT

In this text, Gordon Brown, a Scot, tries to convince his readers, the addressee, of his point of view. You will need to examine how he develops his argument. A table, like the one below, can help you do this. Maybe you can link more than one paragraph with just one heading.

Highlight quotes in the text to show how he supports his arguments. Remember that you can use indirect, direct/literal and integrated quotations in your answer. → S3 → S12.4

Line refs.	Heading	Content (notes)
ll.1–9	*Work together or bust*	*opening statement; need for radical change if Scotland not to leave/UK not to break up*
ll.10–30		
ll.31–65		
ll.66–end		

3 EVALUATION As a student from Scotland, write a letter to the editor of *The Guardian* commenting on the former Prime Minister's article in which you express your concerns about UK 'nationalisms' and how they might affect the hopes you have for your future and for the society you would like to be a part of. → S19.1

TIP

Tasks like this give you an opportunity to talk about a number of different themes as they relate to you; e.g. national politics, Brexit, the EU, globalisation, …, not just those mentioned in the text. You can develop and extend your ideas.

OR

You have been invited to speak at an international youth conference in the United Kingdom on the future prospects of young people in Germany. Write a short speech of about 300 words.
→ S15

TIP

Remember that you will be speaking to a group of peers. Try to catch your listeners' attention at the beginning and use rhetorical techniques to get your message across clearly. Give examples and give a short summary of your message at the end.

SUPPORT

Make a list of 5 bullet points for the issues you wish to focus on in your letter/speech.

4 MULTIPLE CHOICE Tick the correct answer. Only one answer is correct.

1. The text deals with the need for …

☐ a) devolution in the United Kingdom.
☐ b) cooperation between the nations and regions.
☐ c) Scottish independence.
☐ d) greater powers for Westminster.

2. The shift in votes that gave the Conservatives an 80-seat majority signals …

☐ a) a country at ease with itself.
☐ b) a newfound unity.
☐ c) a desire for fundamental change.
☐ d) a growing national consensus.

3. The 75-year-old safety net refers to …

☐ a) various charities.
☐ b) food banks.
☐ c) the welfare state.
☐ d) the NHS.

4. The Conservatives have promised to …

☐ a) address economic insecurity.
☐ b) invest in the north.
☐ c) build an airport.
☐ d) put an end to injustice.

5. Gordon Brown says 83 % live in one country. He is referring to the …

☐ a) population.
☐ b) population with an ethnic background.
☐ c) most wealthy people.
☐ d) electorate.

6. The problems common to all parts of the UK are …

☐ a) a deadly mixture.
☐ b) the result of Brexit.
☐ c) like a train out of control.
☐ d) reasons for rising UK nationalism.

5 SENTENCE COMPLETION

1. With the UK's history as a unitary state, giving the outlying nations and regions new decision-making powers would be _____

_____

2. George Orwell said patriots love their country while nationalists _____

_____

3. One benefit of cooperation is _____

_____

6 SEQUENCING Put these points in the order in which they are dealt with in the text. (ll.40–65)

☐ poorly paid jobs
☐ top earners overpaid
☐ north-south economic imbalance
☐ NHS treatment of patients
☐ limited prospects for young people
☐ welfare state in decline
☐ shrinking self-esteem

A1 ◁)) **7 MULTIPLE CHOICE** Listen to a speech about multiculturalism in the UK and tick the correct answer. Only one answer is correct.

1. In the introduction, the moderator points out that Rabina Khan is …

☐ a) a housing officer.
☐ b) a local politician.
☐ c) a poet.
☐ d) an actor.

2. She recently …

☐ a) was awarded an MBE.
☐ b) won a prize.
☐ c) was put forward for an award.
☐ d) was named 'European Muslim Woman of Influence of the year'.

3. According to the moderator, she thinks multiculturalism …

☐ a) needs to be seen in a more differentiated way.
☐ b) is misunderstood by most local politicians.
☐ c) is easy to define.
☐ d) is a positive feature of British society today.

4. Rabina Khan uses the example of Tower Hamlets to show that …

☐ a) the borough is a hotbed of Islamic extremism.
☐ b) multiculturalism has encouraged polarised identities.
☐ c) local people support the English Defence League.
☐ d) the majority of British people support solidarity.

5. Statistics in a recent Demos report show that British Muslims are …

☐ a) less patriotic than most British non-Muslims.
☐ b) sometimes more patriotic than British non-Muslims.
☐ c) as patriotic as British non-Muslims.
☐ d) as patriotic as 83 % of British non-Muslims.

London borough of Tower Hamlets

6. Rabina Khan describes herself as …

☐ a) a product of multiculturalism.
☐ b) a Muslim.
☐ c) a British Muslim.
☐ d) British and Bangladeshi.

8 SHORT ANSWERS Answer the questions in key words.

1. How does "valuing multiple identities" affect multicultural Britain?

_____

2. Compare the identification of British and French Muslims with their country.

_____

3. As a Muslim, how does Rabina Khan see Islamophobia?

_____

4. Having listened to the complete recording, say what Rabina Khan's intention with her speech is.

_____

9 MEDIATION In your English course, you are doing a project called: 'How others see us and we see them.' Your teacher has given you an extract from a German newspaper article about John Kampfner's book, *Why the Germans do it better*, and asked you to write a handout for the other course members in which you summarise what he says about the British and the Germans and their relationship with each other. Highlight the relevant points, using the suggested colour coding, before writing your handout. → S25

Sind die Deutschen die besseren Briten geworden?

Viele Briten verbanden mit Deutschland lange vor allem Hitler und Sauerkraut. Das hat sich geändert. Was steckt hinter der neuen Bewunderung für die Deutschen?

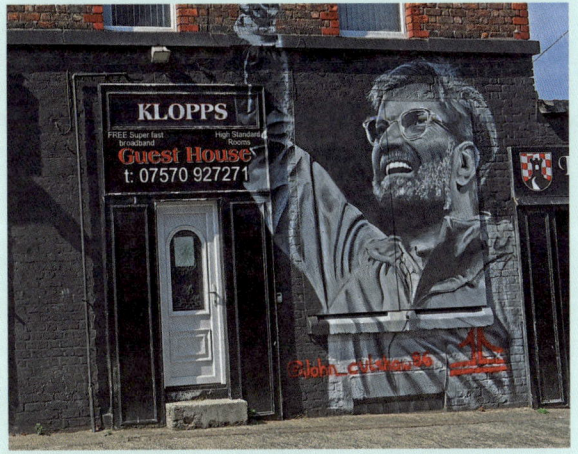

[...] Deutschland ist sexy geworden im Königreich. Kampfners Buch stieg in wenigen Tagen auf die Bestsellerliste der *Sunday Times*, sein Verlag soll Mühe mit dem Nachdrucken haben.
5 Überrascht und überwältigt gab sich der Autor bei seiner Buchpräsentation. Dabei dürfte Kampfner geahnt, zumindest gehofft haben, dass er mit seinem Lob auf Deutschland einen Nerv treffen würde. „Guckt euch dieses Land an,
10 ihr Briten, ihr Amerikaner, und lernt von seiner Bescheidenheit!", rief er aus. Damit sprach er vielen Briten aus der Seele, jedenfalls all denen, die an ihrer Regierung verzweifeln. „Humility", was sich auch als Demut übersetzen lässt, ist
15 nicht die einzige Tugend, die Kampfner den Deutschen bescheinigt, obwohl er diese besonders betont: „Ihr seid so viel besser, als ihr denkt!", ruft er ihnen zu. Kampfner, der in den achtziger Jahren als Korrespondent in Bonn und
20 Ost-Berlin gearbeitet hat und für das Buch noch einmal ausgiebig gereist ist, sieht Deutschland als Modell schlechthin: hart arbeitend, aufs Wesentliche bezogen, sozial zusammenhaltend und ehrlich mit sich selbst, vor allem mit der eigenen
25 Vergangenheit. „Wir im Königreich haben keinen Mangel an Hybris, an ‚Rule, Britannia!', an Arroganz und an Rückblicken auf unsere glorreiche Vergangenheit", sagt er. „Warum lernen wir nicht von der stillen Kompetenz eines anderen
30 Landes?" Stille Kompetenz, das hört man wiederum als Deutscher gerne.

Etwas scheint sich verändert, ja verkehrt zu haben im Verhältnis der Briten und der Deutschen. Lange Zeit, eigentlich bis vor weni-
35 gen Jahren, wurde ja überwiegend andersherum geschwärmt. Generationen von Deutschen betrachteten die Briten als eine Art auserwählte Nation. Man blickte auf zu ihrer Weltläufigkeit, ihrer historischen Sonderstellung, ihrer Rede-
40 gabe, ihrem Humor, ihrem Mut zur Exzentrik. Die Briten machten es vielleicht nicht besser als die Deutschen, aber glamouröser, ausgeruhter, kreativer, selbstbewusster. [...]

Was also ist heute neu? Nimmt man Kampf-
45 ners Buch als Maßstab, könnte man sagen, dass gewachsene Sympathie in nackte Bewunderung umgeschlagen ist. Dies fällt umso stärker auf, als gleichzeitig der Insel-Rausch der Deutschen einem schweren Kater gewichen ist. Paul Lever, der als britischer Botschafter den Regierungs-
50 umzug von Bonn nach Berlin begleitete, macht dieses Wechselspiel an den Medien fest. Die deutsche Berichterstattung über Großbritannien sei in den vergangenen Jahren „toxisch" ge-
55 worden, schrieb er kürzlich in einem Kommentar für das „Royal United Services Institute", dass sich normalerweise mit noch bedeutenderen Fragen der Weltpolitik beschäftigt. Deutsche Medien, schrieb Lever, porträtierten das König-
60 reich als „ein Land, das Mitleid verdient, dessen Führung inkompetent und korrupt ist, dessen demokratische Strukturen zerfallen, dessen Wirtschaft kurz vor dem Zusammenbruch steht und dessen Bevölkerung manipulativ in die
65 Wahl von Extremisten getrieben worden ist".

Im Gegensatz dazu würden britische Zeitungen, die jahrzehntelang Kriegsstereotypen bedient hätten, heute „weitgehend respektvoll und korrekt" über Deutschland berichten. Als
70 Beispiele erwähnt Lever „die weitverbreitete Bewunderung für Deutschlands Wirtschafts- und Sozialsystem, die Effizienz, mit der auf Corona-Pandemie reagiert wurde, und die Qualität der politischen Führung unter Kanzlerin Angela
75 Merkel". [...]

Jochen Buchsteiner, *Frankfurter Allgemeine Zeitung*, 2020

10 WARM-UP Describe, analyse and evaluate the photo on the previous page. Before attempting the task, you can do some internet research about Jürgen Klopp and the influence he has had on the way the British see Germany and the Germans.

TIP

When working with visuals, remember the four steps: • Introduction • Description • Analysis • Evaluation. → S27.1

11 MONOLOGUE Analyse the cartoon taking into consideration the situation in the UK. Then describe the photo to your partner and explain how it relates to the topic presented in your cartoon. → S27

TIP

Look at the reading text written by the former UK Prime Minister Gordon Brown which you have already worked with at the beginning of this workbook topic as well as texts in your *Green Line Oberstufe* textbook. They will have given you background information you can use here.

Partner A

Partner B

SUPPORT

Make brief notes on your cartoon here to use in your presentation and remember the four steps:

1. Introduction (*here*: Issue)

_____

2. Description

_____

_____

3. Analysis

_____

_____

4. Evaluation

_____

_____

12 DIALOGUE You and your partner work in an advertising agency and have been asked to create a poster which draws attention to the plight of the poor in the United Kingdom using one of the four photos here (Tasks 11 and 12). Consider the arguments for and against the photos before choosing by making notes in the table below and then suggest an eye-catching slogan for the poster.

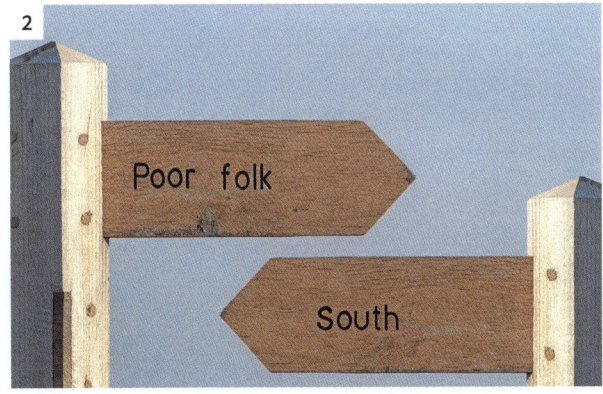

	Pro	Con
Photo A2 (Task 11)		
Photo B2 (Task 11)		
Photo 1 (Task 12)		
Photo 2 (Task 12)		

5 The Englishes

1 MONOLOGUE

Partner A
Describe the cartoon and explain its message. Comment on this English-speaking tourist's method of communication in relation to other possible options.

Partner B
Describe the cartoon and explain its message. Comment on whether the English speaker's attitude to other languages is justifiable.

It's a good thing Chuck raised his voice, because Pedro understood loud English.

"I say to hell with it. If it can't be said in English, it ain't worth saying at all."

2 DIALOGUE

a) Referring to the statistics and quotes, discuss reasons for and consequences of how foreign languages are taught in the EU, the UK and the US.

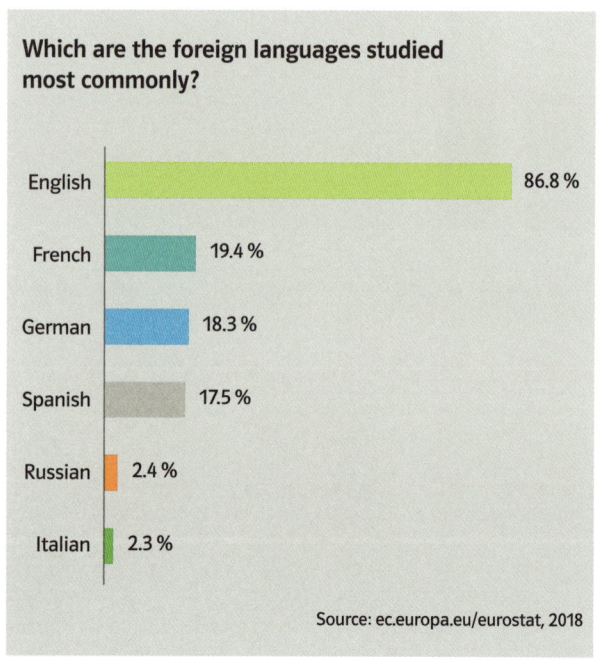

Which are the foreign languages studied most commonly?

Language	%
English	86.8 %
French	19.4 %
German	18.3 %
Spanish	17.5 %
Russian	2.4 %
Italian	2.3 %

Source: ec.europa.eu/eurostat, 2018

> Many European countries mandate that students study more than one foreign language.
>
> Kat Devlin, *Pew Research FactTank*, 2020

> [Only] 20% of [US] K-12 [1] students are enrolled in foreign language classes.
>
> Kat Devlin, *Pew Research FactTank*, 2020

> Language learning: German and French drop by half in UK schools [...] Foreign language learning is at its lowest level in UK secondary schools since the turn of the millennium, with German and French falling the most.
>
> Branwen Jeffreys, *BBC online*, 2019

---

1 K-12 All students in American schools from kindergarten to Year 12, i.e. aged between 4 and 19 years old

b) Briefly discuss why it is important for your own future to learn a foreign language.

c) You have been asked to design a poster or social media meme to attract students to enrol in an English language course at your local college. You may use one of the texts or pictures below or suggest other text or picture ideas. Discuss and try to agree on which picture and text you would use and what would make your poster/meme successful.

3 important reasons to learn English:

1 You can communicate in English all over the world.

2
English is an important skill for getting a job.

3
You have a bigger audience when you publish your work in English.

6 The US – a diverse nation

The legacy of Joe Louis' loss to Max Schmeling on Juneteenth

When one of the world's most famous black Americans, Joe Louis, bludgeoned Germany's Max Schmeling to a first-round defeat in 1938, it was symbolic of free-world endurance against
5 the fascism of Schmeling's Nazi homeland. In two minutes and four seconds of brutal efficiency, Louis exploded with a barrage of uppercuts, crosses and hooks to put his opponent on the canvas three times. [...]
10 In victory, Louis delivered the geopolitical message President Franklin D Roosevelt had called for when the fighter had visited the White House just a few weeks prior. "Joe, we need muscles like yours to beat Germany," the New
15 York Times quoted the president as telling the Brown Bomber ahead of the bout. Hitler had passed the Nuremberg Race Laws a year earlier, the extension of which would soon see black people like Louis, along with Jews and Roma
20 people, categorized as legally inferior to whites within the Reich. The growing boldness of Nazi policy was drawing international condemnation, but for a black man who grew up the son of an Alabama sharecropper and whose family had
25 been harassed by the KKK, the use of colour to distinguish citizen rights was an all too familiar aspect of life in America.

It was a situation reflected by sentiments that surrounded the first meeting between the two
30 fighters at Yankee Stadium, almost-two-years-to-the-day prior to Louis' famous win. "When he fought in 1936, a lot of white America rooted for the German," Joseph Louis Barrow Jr tells the Guardian of his father's challenge. Those who
35 did support Schmeling that day in the Bronx went home happy, as the odds-on-favorite Louis was knocked out in the 12th-round for the first

defeat of his career. "He felt he'd let the entire black race down because he was not supposed to lose that fight. He was supposed to win it, and
40 win it with great applause," Louis Barrow Jr says, speaking from his home in Jacksonville, Florida.

The defeat was all the more significant because it happened on 19 June, a date more recently dubbed Juneteenth to commemorate
45 the day when news of the Emancipation Proclamation reached the people of Galveston, Texas, freeing slaves in the last rebel state. This year will be the first time Juneteenth is marked as an official federal holiday in America, but
50 85 years ago the Louis defeat led to a day of mourning for many black Americans. [...] [In] Louis's prime, his actions in the ring reverberated around the world, as Louis Barrow Jr details in his book Joe Louis: 50 Years an
55 American Hero. "You know, Nelson Mandela, when he came over to the United States after he was freed from Robben Island told me that he, along with thousands of black people in South Africa, had stayed awake to listen to my father's
60 fights on the radio," he wrote. "It provided them with hope." [...]

Beneath the veneer of political narrative however, the reasons for sporting loss can often be far more prosaic. "My father was the
65 invincible Joe [who was 22 at the time] fighting a man eight years older," says Louis Barrow Jr. "It resulted in him not preparing to fight the way he should have. He was spending more time on the golf course." It made Louis' fight to avenge
70 his loss all the more compelling to fight fans of the era. Such was the thirst for action in the 1930s, Louis fought and beat 11 opponents in the two years he waited to meet Schmeling once

Joe Louis' fight with Max Schmeling in 1938

"The Fist": Sculpture of Joe Louis' fist in Detroit

75 again in Yankee Stadium. He took the
heavyweight title from Jack Braddock in 1937
proving the perfect lure for a belt-less Schmeling
to agree to a rematch. [...]

80 Schmeling was held up by Nazi propagandists
as a poster boy of an Aryan race with a sacred
destiny, all of which added to the drama of the
fight which had sold out the 75,000 tickets soon
after being announced. Not that the fighters
involved necessarily shared the polarization of
85 the build-up. "To some it was freedom and
democracy versus fascism, FDR versus Adolf
Hitler. It meant different things to different
people but to Max and my father it was really
just the meeting of two gladiators," says Louis
90 Barrow Jr.

Louis was in the shape of his life and carried
a ferocious hunger into the ring that night. His
win not only avenged the sole loss of this career
to that point, it propelled him into the center of
95 American culture and adoration. "He was on the
front page above the fold of every newspaper,
without killing a white person," Louis Barrow Jr
says of the coverage. "I think all of America
admired him and black America had a special
100 affection." [...] "Many of the civil rights icons said
they were only able to do what they did, because

of my father. [...] I knew John Lewis, the
congressman from Atlanta, [and one of the Big
Six organizers of the 1963 civil rights march on
Washington] and every time I would see him 105
he'd talk about what my father meant to him.
How he was a man who proved to America that
black people were more than just slaves.
Muhammad Ali told me at my father's funeral
that Joe Louis was truly the greatest." [...] 110

A presentation of a special Juneteenth belt
will be made to the local Eagle Academy for
Young Men of Harlem, by former heavyweight
champion Michael Spinks. It will help Spinks to
honor the boxer he "took his jab from," he tells 115
the Guardian via email. For Gleason's Gym owner
Bruce Silverglade, it shows Louis' ability to
inspire the next generation remains potent even
after all of these years. "He may be a boxer from
a time gone by, but he crossed cultural divisions 120
during a tough time in the United States," says
Silverglade. "White people promoted him. He
transcended the racial barriers because he was
a hero. Boxing is a sport that crosses barriers, the
kids in my gyms are all shapes and sizes and 125
colors, from all different backgrounds. All
humans trying to do the same thing, and figures
like Joe Louis bring people together."

Ben Wyatt, *The Guardian*, 2020

9 the canvas the floor of the boxing ring • **16 the Brown Bomber** Joe Louis' nickname • **16 bout** a boxing match • **34 the Guardian** a British daily newspaper • **46 the Emancipation Proclamation** the order issued by President Lincoln to abolish slavery in 1865 • **77 belt** a boxing champion is given a belt with a special medal or buckle • **86 FDR** the initials of President Franklin Delano Roosevelt

→ To practise with closed reading comprehension tasks, go to tasks 4–5.

1 COMPREHENSION Summarise the significance of Joe Louis' fights with Max Schmeling.

SUPPORT

1. From memory, note down key ideas on Joe Louis' boxing and his importance to other people.
2. Skim the text to check on your key ideas. Add additional information that is important; do not include unimportant detail.
3. Plan to present ideas in chronological order.
4. Make a note of the main idea in the text for your introduction and an idea for the conclusion that represents the text's message.

2 ANALYSIS Examine the writer's use of references and quotations in the text. The useful phrases might help you.

USEFUL PHRASES

to emphasise • to underline • to highlight (an idea, an aspect) • to refer to • a reference to • a quotation from

SUPPORT

1. Make sure you understand the difference between a reference and a quotation.
2. Underline or highlight all references and quotations in the text. Find a way of categorising them, e.g. famous politicians, sports stars, etc.
3. Note down a sentence explaining the purpose of each reference or quotation.

3 **EVALUATION** Discuss the role of sports in relations between individuals and communities in the US and other countries. Include ideas from the text and from your own experience in your text.

SUPPORT

Step 1   Understand the assignment and get a grasp of your topic
You are going to discuss, assess or evaluate a topic and reach an informed conclusion at the end. When you are asked to discuss, assess or evaluate an issue, you weigh arguments for as well as against it before stating your opinion. For the evaluation task above:
a) Start with an empty sheet or blank screen and a time limit. Note ideas associated with the topic.
 • What do sports mean for the individual – and for you personally? What can you learn from sports?
 • What do sports mean to the nation you live in? Is this meaning unique? Is it different in the US?
 • What is the importance of sports in international competitions?
 • Sum up the example in the text.
 • What examples of famous sports personalities are there? What influence do they have?
 • What problems are there in professional sports?
 • Your opinion: On balance, are sports beneficial to individuals and society?
b) Reread your notes and categorise your ideas. Colours are useful in this process.

Step 2   Structure your arguments
Order your arguments and the supporting evidence. Here you can start with the importance of sports to young people, followed by the importance of sports in your country and then in other countries. You might move on to the example in the text, then add examples of sports in international competitions.

Step 3   Write a captivating introduction → S12
Introductions have to attract the readers' attention – even in academic texts. Use the evidence you have collected to write the introduction to your argumentative essay; for example, a question about the idea behind the Olympic Games. Briefly summarise the issue and announce how you are going to approach it.

Step 4   Write the body and the conclusion → S12
Write the main part of your text, using the structure you prepared. Support your arguments with specific evidence and write paragraphs of roughly equal length. In your conclusion, present a balanced and neutral assessment of the question, leaving the reader with a new thought to consider. Check your argumentative essay.

Marcus Rashford, footballer and activist against racism and for supporting schoolchildren from low-income families

Megan Rapinoe, footballer and activist for LGBT rights

Joe Louis, boxer and symbolic figure for the civil rights movement

4 MULTIPLE CHOICE Tick the correct answers. Only one answer is correct.

1. Joe Louis met the US President at the White House …

   ☐ a) after his fight with Schmeling.

   ☐ b) before he beat Schmeling.

   ☐ c) to make a statement about Germany.

2. When Louis first fought Schmeling, many Americans …

   ☐ a) expected Schmeling to win.

   ☐ b) thought Louis had let their country down.

   ☐ c) were pleased when the German won.

3. The day Louis lost to Schmeling was …

   ☐ a) the anniversary of the end of slavery.

   ☐ b) a new national holiday in the US.

   ☐ c) eighty-five years after the last slaves were set free.

4. Louis Barrow Jr. says his father lost to Schmeling because he …

   ☐ a) spent too much time getting ready for the fight.

   ☐ b) thought too little about his opponent.

   ☐ c) was too young to be world champion.

5. To the two boxers, the second fight …

   ☐ a) meant the same as it did to everyone else.

   ☐ b) was an important political statement

   ☐ c) was no more than a boxing match.

6. People who fought for the interests of African-Americans said that Joe Louis …

   ☐ a) helped to plan civil rights marches in the 1960s.

   ☐ b) took part in a major protest in Washington DC.

   ☐ c) was an important example for their campaign.

5 TRUE OR FALSE Mark which of these statements are true or false and give evidence from the text quoting a short phrase.

Statement	True	False	Evidence
1. In 1938, Joe Louis won the fight against Max Schmeling very quickly.			
2. As a successful boxer, Louis had little experience of racism in the US.			
3. Many people thought Louis might lose the fight against Schmeling in 1936.			
4. People in other countries couldn't follow Louis' boxing matches.			
5. Louis became a boxing champion before his second fight with Schmeling.			
6. When Louis fought Schmeling again, he was fitter than he had ever been.			
7. Boxer Michael Spinks says that Louis inspired his boxing technique.			
8. According to the text, Louis is still influential.			

A1 🔊 **6** **SHORT ANSWERS** You will hear an interview from 2016 with Kareem Abdul-Jabbar, who is talking about political activism in sport. While listening, fill in the missing information, writing **1 to 10** words or numbers.

TIP

Exam practice
Try doing these tasks in strict exam conditions, for example using these rules:
You will hear the recording **twice**. You have **1 minute** to look at the task.
You will have **30 seconds** to finalise your answers after the second listening.

Time	Person	What they were/did
during the Vietnam War/ in the 1960s	Kareem Abdul-Jabbar Muhammad Ali	
in 1968	Abdul-Jabbar Abdul-Jabbar	
in 2016	Colin Kaepernick Abdul-Jabbar	

7 **MULTIPLE CHOICE** Tick the correct answer. There is only one correct answer.

1. Referring to Colin Kaepernick, Kareem Abdul-Jabbar says …
   - ☐ a) the footballer has risked too much.
   - ☐ b) his protest deserves appreciation.
   - ☐ c) people should follow his example.

2. According to Abdul-Jabbar, athletes reacting to a controversial issue…
   - ☐ a) should not make people angry.
   - ☐ b) need to avoid damage to their future in sport.
   - ☐ c) have to make a personal decision.

3. After the shooting of Martin Luther King, people felt that Abdul-Jabbar should…
   - ☐ a) just be happy with his chance for success in sport.
   - ☐ b) do more than just stand in protest.
   - ☐ c) not be allowed to play professional sport.

4. According to the interview, one thing that Abdul-Jabbar and Kaepernick have in common is …
   - ☐ a) having the chance to explain their views in the media.
   - ☐ b) being told to leave the US and live elsewhere.
   - ☐ c) their patriotism and love of their home country.

5. When Muhammad Ali refused to serve in the military, Abdul-Jabbar …
   - ☐ a) took action to get African Americans' support for Ali.
   - ☐ b) supported Ali by refusing to go to Vietnam.
   - ☐ c) joined other sports personalities to help Ali.

6. Abdul-Jabbar says that his actions have …
   - ☐ a) always helped people to start talking about issues.
   - ☐ b) sometimes helped others to understand issues better.
   - ☐ c) usually helped him to understand issues better.

8 MEDIATION You are working on a project entitled 'International Perspectives: Views from Abroad', which has a website aimed primarily at students at schools and universities across Europe. You have found the following information in a blog and are to write an article about the writer's ideas on moving to the US, focusing on working life and getting on with people there. Write your article, with a suitable headline.

Leben in den USA – Das alltägliche Leben

Auch wenn die USA [und] Deutschland wirtschaftlich und kulturell gesehen relativ ähnlich sind [...], ist das Leben in den USA doch deutlich anders als in Deutschland. Auf den ersten Blick
5 sind es die kleinen Dinge, wie zum Beispiel die breiteren Fahrspuren, die größeren Parkplätze und die größeren Packungen im Supermarkt, die ein Gefühl für die Andersartigkeit des Landes vermitteln. Doch auch das System ist ein ande-
10 res, Krankenversicherung und soziale Absicherung funktionieren in den USA anders als in Deutschland und das gesamte Arbeitsumfeld unterscheidet sich zu dem in Deutschland. [...]

Um als Auswanderer in den USA eine Chance
15 zu haben, ist ein Hochschulabschluss von Vorteil oder eine Ausbildung zu einer spezialisierten Fachkraft. Akademiker und Fachkräfte werden in den USA am dringendsten gesucht, wer schon einen Job hat wenn er umzieht, hat es deutlich
20 leichter ein Visum zu bekommen, als Arbeitssuchende. Viele Auswanderer nehmen das Arbeiten in den USA als viel eigenverantwortlicher wahr als in Deutschland und sehen dort beruflich mehr Möglichkeiten. Das häufige Wechseln
25 des Arbeitsplatzes wird dort weniger als Manko gewertet als in Deutschland und auch ältere Arbeitnehmer haben noch Chancen, einen Job zu finden.

Wer mit Durchsetzungsvermögen und einem
30 klaren Ziel vor Augen in die USA kommt, hat in den USA immer noch sehr gute Chancen es weit zu schaffen. Aufstiege sind in den USA schneller möglich als in Deutschland, nicht umsonst gelten die USA auch als das Land der unbegrenzten
35 Möglichkeiten. Allerdings steht den vielen Möglichkeiten und der größeren Eigenverantwortung auch eine schlechtere soziale Absicherung gegenüber, die man bereit sein muss in Kauf zu nehmen. [...]
40 So gibt es Arbeitslosengeld in den USA nur dann, wenn man seinen Job ohne eigenes Verschulden verloren hat. Wer selber kündigt oder eine Kündigung durch Fehlverhalten provoziert hat, erhält keine Unterstützung. Auch Personen,
45 die selbstständig sind oder in Teilzeit oder Zeitarbeitsverträgen arbeiten, erhalten kein Arbeitslosengeld. Arbeitslosengeld wird in der Regel für sechs Monate ausbezahlt, die Regelungen variieren aber von Staat zu Staat. [...]

Jedes Angestelltenverhältnis in Deutschland 50 sieht mindestens 24 Tage bezahlten Urlaub pro Jahr als gesetzliches Minimum vor (bei einer Vollzeit-Stelle). [...] In den USA ist bezahlter Urlaub immer noch ein Fremdwort in vielen Firmen und Arbeitnehmer müssen sich ihren 55 Urlaub häufig unbezahlt nehmen. [...]

Je nach Region variieren die Lebenshaltungskosten in den USA stark. Während Mieten in Manhattan nahezu unbezahlbar hoch sind, sind Häuser auf dem Land im Mittleren Westen rela- 60 tiv günstig. [...] Im Supermarkt sind die Kosten für Lebensmittel auch etwas höher als in Deutschland, gerade was Obst und Gemüse angeht. Auch die anderen Lebensmittel des täglichen Bedarfs wie Milch, Käse und Brot sind et- 65 was teurer. Hier hängt es ebenfalls wieder davon ab, in welcher Stadt oder Region man sich befindet und auch, wie hoch die jeweilige Steuer dort ist. [...]

Wer in die USA auswandert verlässt sein sozi- 70 ales Umfeld zu Hause und steht im neuen Land erst einmal ziemlich alleine da. [...] Offenheit ist die wichtigste Voraussetzung, um Leute kennenzulernen und neue Freundschaften zu schließen. Vorurteile haben dabei nichts verloren und 75 wichtig ist es auch zu akzeptieren, dass Amerikaner einen anderen kulturellen Hintergrund haben als Deutsche. [...] So ist es Teil der amerikanischen Kultur Small Talk zu betreiben und auch aus Höflichkeit zu sagen „Lass uns doch 80 mal zusammen etwas unternehmen". Das ist nicht immer ernst gemeint, sondern kann eben auch eine höfliche Floskel sein, ebenso wie sich auf die Frage „How are you?", also „Wie geht's?", die Teil der amerikanischen Begrüßungskultur 85 ist, nicht direkt alle Sorgen von der Seele geredet werden sollten. [...] Es kann nicht oft genug betont werden, dass es unheimlich wichtig ist in den USA erst einmal Urlaub zu machen, bevor man dauerhaft dorthin zieht. Auch wenn es für 90 viele als das absolute Traumland erscheint hat es auch seine Schattenseiten [...] Blauäugig drauf los zu fliegen ist keine gute Idee, sondern sowohl das Land als auch die spezielle Region in die es einen zieht, sollte vorher gut bekannt 95 sein.

Hanna Lose and Selina Möhring, *USA Tipps* website, 2021

9 MONOLOGUE Depending on whether you want to practise speaking about one picture or two, choose one of the following options. → S27.2

Partner A

Either:

Choose cartoon 1 or 2.

Cartoon 1: Describe the cartoon and explain its message. Relate the message to different times in US history.

Cartoon 2: Describe the cartoon and explain its message. Comment on the issues addressed in the cartoon.

OR

Describe both cartoons (1 and 2). Explain their messages and what they have in common.

Partner B

Either:

Choose cartoon 3 or 4.

Cartoon 3: Describe the cartoon and explain the point the artist is making about constitutional rights. Assess its effectiveness.

Cartoon 4: Describe the cartoon and explain the event it refers to. Comment on the message of the cartoon.

OR

Describe both cartoons (3 and 4). Explain their messages and comment on the points that are made about the Constitution.

"The government is comin' to take away our freedom. Barricade yourself inside, Marge, and stay there 'til I tell you."

" 'Life, liberty, and the pursuit of the almighty dollar' is too long. Let's change it to 'happiness'. "

10 DIALOGUE Imagine you are in the US as an exchange student. Your class is planning a campaign for greater justice in society. Discuss with your partner which of the following ideas would be most effective for your campaign. Try to agree on the two best ideas.

leaflets for local residents   a summer festival with information for visitors

an interview for local radio   emails to the state government

a social media campaign   large roadside posters

OR

11 DIALOGUE There are numerous people trying to enter the US in the hope of a better life. They are a factor in the workforce, but some see them as a problem and support stricter measures to stop people immigrating. Choose one of the following roles and discuss the issue of immigration, presenting the arguments in your role. You may begin by discussing the statistics, "Dreamers' rights?".

Partner A
is in favour of stricter immigration policy. Ideas to consider include …
- the cost of public services
- the influence of 'foreign' cultures
- the need for stricter laws and tighter border controls
- the deportation of undocumented immigrants ('illegals') in the US

Partner B
is in favour of a more lenient immigration policy. Ideas to consider include …
- immigrants in the work force
- the advantages of multiculturalism
- problems with stricter laws and border controls
- citizenship for undocumented immigrants ('illegals') in the US

USEFUL PHRASES

Language tips for role play

Explaining ideas:
One reason (for this) is … • One point to consider is … • Obviously, this is because … • The idea behind this is (that) …

Commenting on both sides of an issue:
You might think that … but … • Some people say that … but … • It's often said that … but it seems to me that …

Reacting to/Bringing in your partner:
Ah! I see what you mean. • I'm not sure what you're getting at. • The problem is (that) … • … is a good idea, isn't it?

Explaining or correcting yourself:
What I mean is … • That's not quite what I meant.
Concluding negotiations:
That's one thing we can agree on, but … •

When you're stuck:
Oh! I've forgotten what I was going to say! • What's the word? It's on the tip of my tongue…

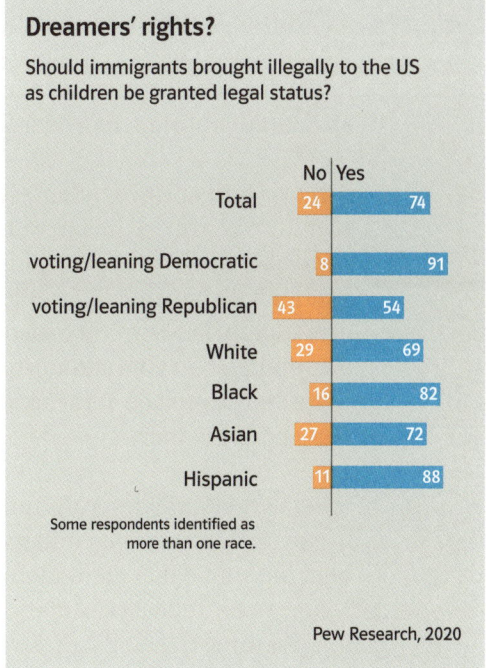

Dreamers' rights?

Should immigrants brought illegally to the US as children be granted legal status?

	No	Yes
Total	24	74
voting/leaning Democratic	8	91
voting/leaning Republican	43	54
White	29	69
Black	16	82
Asian	27	72
Hispanic	11	88

Some respondents identified as more than one race.

Pew Research, 2020

7 International relations

1 MEDIATION In an international internet forum you have read a post in which someone argues that the hunger people still suffer from in some developing countries has nothing to do with people in industrialised countries and that it is only the individual governments which are responsible. As you have recently read an article about hunger by the German *Welthungerhilfe* (see the text below), you do not agree. Write a blog post in which you outline to what extent foreign countries contribute to cause hunger.

Die Ursachen des Hungers

Alle zehn Sekunden stirbt ein Kind unter fünf Jahren an den Folgen von Hunger. 690 Millionen Menschen hungern, zwei Milliarden leiden an Mangelernährung. Dabei gibt es genug Nahrung,
5 Wissen und Mittel für alle. Mehr noch: Alle Menschen haben ein Recht auf Nahrung. Die Welthungerhilfe arbeitet seit ihrer Gründung mit vielfältigen Strategien daran, den Hunger in der Welt bis 2030 zu beenden.

10 **Warum gibt es Hunger?** Die Ursachen von Hunger und Mangelernährung sind vielfältig. Die Agenda 2030 zeigt den Weg in eine gerechte Welt. Die Welthungerhilfe konzentriert sich dabei auf ihr Kernthema Ernährungssicherung.

15
Naturkatastrophen: Wetterextreme haben seit jeher zu Hungerkrisen geführt. Dürren oder Überschwemmungen zerstören Ernten. Mit dem Klimawandel nehmen extreme Wetterereignisse zu. Dürren in mehreren aufeinander folgenden
20 Jahren schwächen die Widerstandskraft (Resilienz) der Bevölkerung. Sie müssen ihre Vorräte an Saatgut aufbrauchen oder Vieh schlachten.

Armut: Hunger ist vor allem eine Folge von Armut. Wer arm ist, hat zu wenig Geld für Essen,
25 kann aber auch nicht genug für die eigene Gesundheit sorgen und in die Bildung der Kinder investieren. Frauen sind meist besonders benachteiligt. Nur eine standortgerechte Landwirtschaft kann den Teufelskreis von Armut und
30 Hunger überwinden.

Kriege und Konflikte: Aufgrund bewaffneter Auseinandersetzungen müssen Menschen fliehen und sind daher nicht mehr in der Lage, ihre
35 Felder zu bestellen. Häufig verlieren sie ihr gesamtes Hab und Gut. Straßen und landwirtschaftliche Infrastruktur wie Bewässerungsanlagen werden zerstört. Durch die eingeschränkte Sicherheit leidet auch der Handel,
40 Nahrungsmittel werden rar und teuer.

Ungleichheit: Die Agenda 2030 ruft uns dazu auf, niemanden zurückzulassen. Trotzdem verschärft sich die Ungleichheit zwischen Arm und Reich, sowohl global als auch innerhalb der einzelnen Länder. Ein Prozent der Weltbevölkerung 45 besitzt fast die Hälfte des Weltvermögens. Die „untere Milliarde" der Armen und Hungernden hat kaum eine Chance, sich aus ihrer Misere zu befreien. Der Food Security Standard (FSS) soll die Ernährungssicherheit durch mehr Gerech- 50 tigkeit weltweit überwachen.

Verzerrter Welthandel: Die reichen Staaten bestimmen die Regeln der internationalen Politik. Unfaire Handelsabkommen und Subventionen schaffen Marktzugänge und Preisvorteile für 55 Unternehmen aus den Industrienationen. Entwicklungsländer exportieren vor allem Rohstoffe, die Gewinne schöpfen reiche Staaten ab. Ein gerechter Agrarhandel fördert kleinbäuerliche Landwirt/innen sowie die ländliche Wertschöp- 60 fung (Value Chains). Die Welthungerhilfe gibt den benachteiligten Hauptproduzent/innen von Nahrungsmitteln eine Stimme.

Schlechte Regierungsführung:

65 Die Regierungen in Entwicklungsländern richten ihre Politik meist nicht an den Bedürfnissen der ärmsten Bevölkerung aus. Es fehlen Strategien, die Landwirtschaft im eigenen Land so zu fördern, dass niemand mehr hungern
70 muss. Korruption ist eines der größten Entwicklungshemmnisse, Landraub ein großes Problem.

Ressourcenverschwendung und Klimawandel:
Wenn alle Menschen so lebten wie die reichen Länder, wären Ressourcen wie Wasser und Böden bald verbraucht. Die Folgen haben andere zu 75 tragen: Ausbreitung von Wüsten, Bodenerosion, Wasserknappheit und extreme Wetterphänomene als Folge des Klimawandels machen sich vor allem in den Ländern bemerkbar, die ohnehin an Hunger und Armut leiden. 80

From the Welthungerhilfe website, 2021

2 EVALUATION Choose one of the following writing tasks:
The man on the right who voices his doubts about the success of the conference (e.g. on trade or climate change) is the chairman of the meeting. In an opening speech, he addresses the problems he foresees and attempts to win the participants over for his view of international cooperation.
Write his introductory speech. → S15

"I have grave doubts about the success of this conference."

OR

The picture makes an analogy between international relations and a game (of chess or checkers).
Discuss to what extent this analogy is true.

8 India

Screenplay *Lion* by Luke Davies

Adapted from the autobiographic novel *A long way home* by Saroo Brierley.

Saroo is a boy from India who wrote a novel as an adult about his life that started in India. He grows up in an Indian village with his older brother, his younger sister and his mother. They don`t have much money, and his mother and brother work hard to provide for them. This scene is about his Indian home as a young boy.

(Int. one-room home – soon after (evening). Home is a dirt-floor shack. Kerosene lamp. Bare walls. Coal fire in the corner. Plastic dish tub. Subsistence living. Saroo's mother (Kamla, 30 – beautiful, but
5 *lined by life) ladles dhal onto plates for Saroo, Guddu, and Shekila (2). Kallu (a boy, 9 – Saroo and Guddu's brother, cheeky, flighty) enters, sits, unwrapping a cloth containing scraps of bread.)*

Kallu I got the bread!
10 **Saroo** *(it's competitive)* We got the milk!
(They devour the meal in silence. We study each person. Kamla unties the plastic bag, pours the milk into a bowl. She dips a crust of bread and gives it to Shekila to suckle on. Guddu, Kallu, and
15 *Saroo take a sip each and pass the bowl. Saroo offers the bowl to his mother. She smiles a gentle No. Saroo grins at Guddu. So proud of their milk escapade. Kallu ups and leaves as fast as he came.)*

(Int. one-room home – soon after (evening). Saroo
20 *lies with Shekila on her little "cot" – barely a scrap of mattress – on the floor. Soothing her, stroking her head.)*

Saroo Shhh. Shhh.
(Saroo lifts his head, looks at Kamla as she drapes
25 *her head with a silk sari and begins to head out. She looks back at his questioning little face.)*
Kamla You know I have to work.

One night at the age of five, while his mother and brother are working, he is separated from them and ends up in an orphanage. When Saroo is six years old, he is adopted by an Australian couple who want to help children from abroad. Years later he wants to find his original family in India and tries to link pictures in his mind and words and names he remembers to maps. His girlfriend Lucy is exhausted as he is by his search.

(Ext. street outside, Luke's place – continuous (night). Saroo just wants to get away. Lucy
30 *follows.)*

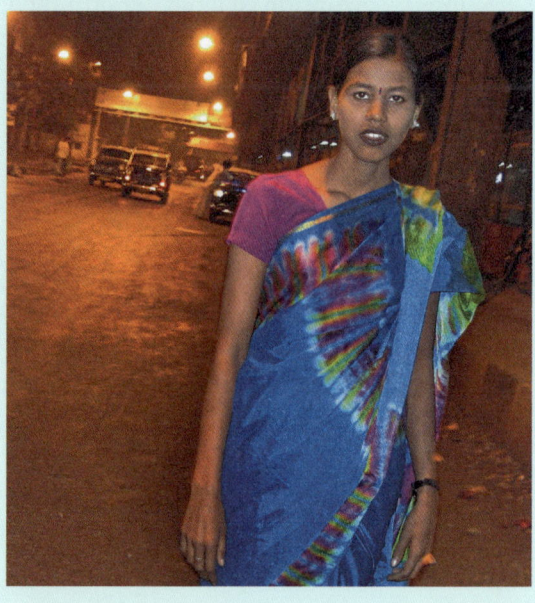

Lucy Don't do this.
Saroo You don't get it.
Lucy You have to face reality.
Saroo What do you mean, "reality"? 35
Lucy The reality that you're ruining your life! That you're not even here!
Saroo Do you have any idea what it's like, knowing my real brother and mother spend every day of their lives looking for me? 40
Lucy *(genuinely bewildered)* What?
Saroo How every day they scream my name. *(beat)* And I feel their touch. I see their faces. Can you imagine the pain they must be in, not knowing where I am? Twenty-five years, Luce. 45 Twenty-five!
Lucy Why haven't you ever told me this was happening?
Saroo And we swan about in our privileged lives. Pretending. It makes me sick. 50
(Lucy is speechless.)
Lucy *(faint, soft)* I never stopped you ... *(It's as if Saroo suddenly sees her pain properly. And is brought back to earth. The air in him deflating.)*
Saroo Listen –. Lucy –. I'm sorry –. I can't do 55 this –. *(beat)* You deserve more –.
Lucy – don't! Don't you dare.
(Her eyes fill with tears.)
Lucy *(CONT'D)* This is on you! Not me. 60

(Saroo can't deal with her pain. He takes off. This time, she doesn't follow.)

(Ext. Hobart Streets – night.)

(Saroo walks the streets like a tormented soul.
65 *He can't live in two worlds at once. He has to choose. Slowly, his despair becomes defiance. He's made his choice.)*

(Imagined memory, Khandwa streets)
(Kamla wanders the streets, distressed.)
Kamla   Saroo!
(Jump cuts.)
(She's beside herself. Searching empty laneways.)

From: Luke Davies, *Lion*, 2015

---

1 Int int. means that the following scene is set inside; in the interior of a location • **3 subsistence** maintaining or supporting oneself at a minimal level • **5 to ladle** to serve, to spoon, to fill • **5 dhal** an Indian dish made of red lentils and coconut milk and spices • **18 to up** to move upward quickly • **28 Ext.** refers to a place outside; the exterior • **55 (beat)** used in screenwriting to signal a brief pause in a speech or action • **58 (CONT'D)** means in a screenplay the continuation of an interrupted dialogue

→ To practise closed reading comprehension tasks, go to tasks 5–6.

1 COMPREHENSION State the theme of the text.

2 ANALYSIS Write a characterisation of Saroo.

SUPPORT

1. Oftentimes students start to write right away and wonder about bad marks despite good ideas and analysis skills. The reason they fail is that they do not plan and structure their text in advance. Here is how you can do it: Thinking and planning according to a paragraph structure will help you in every subject in every exam. Write the structure below on a separate sheet of paper, read the text or think about your ideas and take notes. You may insert lines to quote the text here. Every task and text might require you to adjust your structure.

   • Introduction
   • What you know about the character: appearance, job, story, family?
   • Actions
   • Emotions/feelings
   • Concluding paragraph

2. Now use this structure (or use the one you have copied down) as you read the screenplay. Collect ideas and jot down notes next to the paragraph symbols and think of linking words to connect your thoughts. Then write the characterisation. Exchange your texts with two classmates for peer editing.

3 ANALYSIS
a) Further practice: Think about your favourite movie or your favourite fictional protagonist. Write a characterisation using your pre-plan-structure without mentioning either the name of the movie or the name of the character.
Plan your structure here:

_____

_____

_____

_____

_____

_____

_____

b) Read your characterisations in class and guess who the texts refer to.

4 EVALUATION

a) Write a letter or an email to either the author or the protagonist Saroo Brierley. Comment on his decision to find his family of origin and to write a book about it.

SUPPORT

1. Do you remember the formalities of a letter's structure? Check Skill 19.4 (Personal letter or email) in your student's book.
2. How should you structure a letter? Check the ideas below. What do you think?

Salutation: _____

Reason for writing/introduction: _____

_____

What you liked: _____

_____

_____

What you disliked/what you would like to ask: _____

_____

_____

Concluding paragraph: _____

3. Write your letter to Saroo. Use the structure above to fill in notes and ideas before you start to write. If you prefer a different paragraph structure, use an extra sheet of paper and adapt the structure above to your notes.

b) Discuss to what extent reading fiction, autobiographies or film scripts can help students understand a foreign country such as India.

SUPPORT

You can also use this paragraph structure for an argumentative essay:

Introduction _____

Pro _____

_____

Con _____

_____

Conclusion _____

TIP

Decide whether you want to argue in favour of or against the statement and swap the order of your pro and con paragraphs accordingly (the side you tend towards should be the last one).

5 SENTENCE COMPLETION Complete the sentences and give a text reference to prove your assertions.

1. Saroo's mother Kamla looks _____

2. For dinner Saroo's family has _____

3. Kamla gives Shekila _____

4. Kamla is a caring and selfless mother because _____

   _____

5. The siblings respect and care for each other because _____

   _____

6. Saroo comforts _____

   _____

7. At night the children are alone because _____

6 TRUE OR FALSE Decide whether the statements are true or false. Tick the correct box and provide a reference from the text to support your answer: Write down the line number(s) plus the first three words and the last three words of the passage to support the solution you have chosen.

	True	False
Example: The screenplay was written by Saroo Brierley. *Line(s): Title "Screenplay 'Lion' written by Luke Davies."*		X
1. Lucy accuses Saroo of losing himself to his mania of the past. _____		
2. Saroo feels well understood by his girlfriend. _____		
3. Saroo feels relieved that he has grown up in a developed country like Australia. _____		
4. Saroo decides to separate from Lucy. _____		
5. Saroo is haunted by the suffering his mother had to go through when he disappeared. _____		

A1 ◁)) **7** TABLE COMPLETION You will hear a radio report about the Indian dish Biryani. While listening, fill in the missing information (if not specified. one aspect is enough). Write a few words or numbers.

TIP

Exam practice
Try doing these tasks in strict exam conditions, for example by adhering to these rules:
You will hear the recording twice. You have one minute to look at the task.
You will then have 30 seconds to finalise your answers after the second listening.

Example: What is Biryani?	_A famous Muslim dish_
1. What are the ingredients? (3 items)	
2. When do people eat it?	
3. How do the chefs keep their recipes a secret? (2 items)	
4. a) Where are the women? (2 items)	
b) Why are the women there?	
5. Where does the interview take place?	
6. Which immigrants are mentioned? (name 4)	
7. When was the eatery established?	
8. What food don't they sell?	
9. Why is it important for the interviewee to speak English well? (2 items)	

8 MEDIATION Your Indian school exchange partner Aashi asked you in your last call what the German media tells you about animal rights in India. So you started to do some research and came across the article "Aus dem Leben einer Heiligen". Outline the situation of cows in India as depicted in the text and write an email to Aashi. → S21

Aus dem Leben einer Heiligen

Jeder weiß, dass in Indien Kühe heilig sind. Kaum einer weiß dagegen, dass ihr Verkauf ein boomendes Geschäft ist. „In demselben Land, in dem die Kuh angebetet wird, will man ihre
5 Milch, ihr Fell und ihr Fleisch", kritisiert eine Aktivistin. Mit beiden Vorderhufen steht die Kuh auf einem Müllhaufen. Mit ihrer feuchten Schnauze stupst sie alte Zeitungen beiseite, schiebt Ziegelsteine weg und knabbert probe-
10 halber an Plastiktüten. Schließlich findet sie einen Blumenkohlstrunk.

Sie ist noch jung, zwischen ihren Hinterbeinen baumelt ein kleines Euter mit unbenutzten rosa Zitzen. Eine von vielen Straßenkühen, die
15 allein durch die Millionenstadt Delhi bummeln. Vor einem winzigen Laden für Stoffe, Garn und Knöpfe gießt ein junger Mann Wasser in einen weißen Plastikeimer. Für die Kühe, die hier vorbeikommen. „Eine Menge Kühe kommen zum
20 Trinken. Deshalb der Eimer. Immer wenn ich Tee mache, fülle ich auch den Eimer."

Auch unsere Kuh senkt ihren Kopf in den Eimer und schlabbert das Wasser in sich hinein. Anket Balashwa geht zurück in seinen Laden,
25 setzt sich auf einen Stuhl, legt die Beine auf den Tresen und nippt an seinem Tee. Eine alte Frau in einem grünen Sari kommt zur Kuh geeilt, holt zwei Rotis aus einer Tüte, kleine Fladenbrote, und hält sie der Kuh hin. Die Kuh hebt den Kopf,
30 umschlingt mit ihrer großen lila Zunge die Brote und kaut bedächtig darauf herum.

Die Frau berührt mit ihren Fingerspitzen erst den Kopf der Kuh und dann ihre eigene Stirn, als wolle sie sich segnen. Seit Jahrtausenden gilt die
35 Kuh in der hinduistischen Mythologie als das heiligste Tier. Die Frau murmelt ein kurzes Gebet, verneigt sich vor der Kuh und geht wieder.

„Jeden Tag stellst du Wasser raus oder Fladenbrot, aber niemand möchte mehr tun als das.
40 Deshalb geht's mit Kühen bergab." Anket Balashwa ist gläubiger Hindu. Der 26-Jährige glaubt, wenn er den Kühen hilft, dann helfen ihm die Götter. Der Kuh wirft er noch einen besorgten Blick hinterher, wie sie über die Straße trottet,
45 und die ewig drängelnden Mopeds, Rikschas und Autos zum Bremsen zwingt. „Es gibt soviel Verkehr in Delhi. Und wenn die Kühe herumstreunen, gibt es Unfälle."

Von den Gläubigen bekommt sie immer wieder ein Fladenbrot zugeworfen. Von solchen 50 Almosen lebt sie. Tag für Tag. […]

In Indien gibt es viele Religionen, 13 Prozent sind Moslems, und drei Prozent Christen, aber sie verletzen mit ihren Essgewohnheiten die religiösen Gefühle der hinduistischen Mehrheit, 55 und zu der gehört Gian Chand Kanjhlia. „Das Schlachten von Kühen ist gesetzlich verboten, das Essen von Kuhfleisch ist nicht verboten. Hindus essen kein Kuhfleisch. Andere Gemeinschaften schon, wie Christen oder Moslems. 60 Und manche Leute schlachten Kühe." […]

Maneka Gandhi im eleganten rosa Sari ist die Vorsitzende von „People for Animals", der größten Tierschutzorganisation Indiens. Außerdem ist sie eine erfolgreiche Politikerin einer hinduis- 65 tischen Partei. Sechsmal war sie Ministerin und hat selbst rigorose Tierschutzgesetze erlassen. Verbittert muss sie mit ansehen, wie der Kuhschutz mit Füßen getreten wird. „Es gibt 10000 Schlachthäuser. Legale und illegale. Alle 70 exportieren Rindfleisch. Letztes Jahr waren es 8,6 Millionen Tonnen. Welche Kuh kann das überleben?" Außerdem werden massenhaft Kühe ins muslimische Nachbarland Bangladesch geschmuggelt, erzählt Maneka Gandhi 75 mit wütendem Blick. Zusammengepfercht auf LKWs oder über die grüne Grenze. […]

Der Widerspruch im Umgang mit Kühen, hat sich im modernen Indien dramatisch verschärft, seufzt Maneka Gandhi und streicht sich ener- 80 gisch eine Haarsträhne hinters Ohr, als rüste sie sich für einen Kampf. „Die Kuh wird gerade mächtig angegriffen. In demselben Land, in dem die Kuh angebetet wird, will man ihre Milch, ihr Fell und ihr Fleisch." 85

Unsere Straßenkuh bummelt weiter durch die Stadt, immer auf der Suche nach etwas Fressbarem. Auch ein Passant bleibt stehen und mustert die Kuh. Sucht er auch nach Fressbarem? Schätzt er gerade ihr Schlachtgewicht 90 und ihren Marktwert?

Gerhard Richter, *Deutschlandradio*, 2017

9 BEFORE YOU START

a) Practise by preparing a one-minute speech about the most interesting topic in this chapter about India. Structure your speech and use linking words: introduction • middle part • finishing up.
You can also use flashcards or notes. Practise and check your timing.

b) When everyone is finished, meet outside in the schoolyard, in the assembly hall, or in your classroom. Walk around while listening to the Indian national anthem. When your teacher stops the music, present your speech to the classmate standing closest to you. Keep going several times. When everyone is done, vote for the classmate who did the best job presenting a really interesting topic.

10 MONOLOGUE Describe and analyse the pictures. What topics about India do they emphasise?

Partner A

Partner B

11 DIALOGUE Choose the picture that interests you the most. Which questions arise when you look at it? Name at least three.
Then discuss the most interesting topics about India: What aspects of India do you want to learn more about? How can you go about doing that? What would you like to see or experience in person?

9 Canada and New Zealand

MEDIATION Your English class is doing a project on Canada and every student has to give an oral presentation on a typically Canadian topic. You have come across the German newspaper article below and want to use the information for your presentation on the region of Eeyou Istchee, home of the Cree Indians.

Am Ende der Straße

Eeyou Istchee ist das Land der Cree-Indianer. Die Region liegt im Norden von Quebec, sie ist größer als Deutschland, nur 18 000 Menschen leben hier.

Nach der dritten Landung ahnt man, warum die Cree diese Route den „Milkrun" nennen. Die Flugzeuge der Air Creebec landen tatsächlich an jeder Milchkanne. Jetzt gerade in Waskaganish,
5 das „Wäss Kägga Nisch" ausgesprochen wird. Das ist auch eine Besonderheit an dieser Region: Man muss lernen, wie man ausspricht, bevor man erzählen kann, wohin man will. Wir wollen nordwärts, die ehemalige Pelzhändlerroute ent-
10 lang durch das Gebiet Eeyou Istchee (Ey Ju Is Tschieh), bis die Straße nicht mehr weitergeht.

Victoria wartet neben einem Monstrum von Auto, einem Ford. Die Kühlerhaube reicht ihr bis zur Schulter. Viele fahren hier solche Wa-
15 gen. Die James Bay Road ist zwar eine Art High-way, doch es gibt auf 620 Kilometern keinen Radioempfang, nur eine Tankstelle, dafür ver-kehrsblinde Karibus und ungeteerte Schotter-pisten. „Dies ist keine Kinderreise", warnte ein
20 Reiseführer online. „Es gibt keine Spaßparks. Sie fahren mit einem Auto voller gelangweilter und jammeriger Gören ans Ende der Welt."

Eine Stunde später sitzen wir am Rupert River, der hier breit und gemächlich in die James
25 Bay mündet. Der Tourismusbeauftragte, der uns Waskaganish zeigen sollte, ist nicht da. Seine Stellvertreterin auch nicht. Victoria telefoniert, und wir holen kurzerhand ihren Cousin Wilfred ab. Es gibt immer einen Plan B, sagt sie, alles ist
30 im Fluss – auch eine der Philosophien der Cree. Wilfred erzählt uns, dass hier knapp 1 900 Men-schen wohnen. Er baut im Auftrag der Gemein-schaft Häuser, insgesamt 30 sollen noch dieses Jahr entstehen. Nur die Teerstraßen sind noch
35 nicht fertig, deswegen staubt es auch so. Wir halten an einer vom Wetter mitgenommenen Hütte. Rupert House, der erste Posten der Hud-son Bay Company. Hier meuterte 1611 die Be-satzung von Henry Hudson, weil sie vom Winter
40 und der glücklosen Suche nach der Nordwest-passage die Nase voll hatte. Wir fahren durch triste Straßen. Die Häuser sind schmucklos, die Straßen verwaist.

[...] Am Abend hat der Tourismusbeauftrag-te Tim Whiskeychan Zeit für uns. Er ist eigent-
45 lich ein bekannter Künstler, er hat eine der kana-dischen Zweidollarmünzen gestaltet. [...] Wir sprechen über die Kultur der Cree, hören Musik aus den vierziger Jahren und sollen ihm glauben, dass Neugeborene, wenn man sie mit Froschurin
50 einreibt, ein Leben lang gegen Insektenstiche immun werden. Wir lernen, dass Torfmoos ein Ersatz für Windeln ist. Und dass es „Tallymen" gibt, die sich um die Jagdgebiete kümmern, die hier „Traplines" heißen und unregelmäßig ge-
55 formt sind, damit jede Familie ein bisschen Berg, Tal und Wasser zum Jagen hat.

Am nächsten Tag, nach vielen Stunden Autofahrt, sitzen wir in Wemindji in einem Tipi. Es gehört Stacey Matches und steht hinter sei-
60 nem Haus im Garten. Über einem Feuer kocht Wasser für Labradortee. Wemindji ist eine junge Gemeinde, 40 Prozent der 1 600 Einwohner sind unter 19. Die meisten wohnen in modernen, ein-stöckigen Häusern. Stacey ist noch bei seinen
65 Großeltern aufgewachsen. Er kennt die Bräuche, kann sie lehren, hält Vorträge, und er beherrscht auch die feine Kunst der Schneeschuhherstel-lung. Seine Frau zeigt uns die kunstvoll gearbe-iteten Schuhe. Wir lernen, wie man Mokassins
70 anhand des Fellverlaufs unterscheidet, dass man sie mit Earl-Grey-Tee wieder auffrischt. Doch von der Pelzjagd lebe hier niemand mehr. Wir lernen, dass man sich im Tipi im Uhrzeigersinn bewegt, so wie die Sonne wandert.
75

Auf der anderen Seite des Ortes. Im Haus des „Grand Councils" sind die „Meetings" in vollem Gange. Über alles wird in den verschiedenen Ins-tanzen des Rates gesprochen, denn allen gehört alles. Wir hängen gemeinsam drin, sagt Stepha-
80 nie Georgekish, die mit ihrem Mann Angus im Gemeindezentrum wartet – auf ein Meeting. Sie

führt das Erlebniscamp Shammy Adventures. Bisher waren aber nur Marketingleute da, sagt
85 sie. Viele schreckt die lange Anreise. Vom Highway sind es 130 Kilometer auf Schotter, dann eine Stunde mit dem Boot und noch mal vier Kilometer mit dem Quad. Dafür ist dort aber alles so, wie es sich die Leute vorstellen, wenn
90 sie den Begriff „indigener Tourismus" hören.

[...] Am nächsten Tag geht es weiter nordwärts. Die Straße scheint endlos. Die weiten Wälder ebenfalls. Wir sehen Strauchkiefern, Schwarzfichten, Balsamtannen, Tamaracks.
95 Ab und zu ist der Baumbestand verbrannt. Als wir an Kilometer 470 vorbeifahren, schauen wir angestrengt ins Grün. Angeblich wurden hier die „Tall People" gesehen. Manche nennen sie „Bigfoot" oder „Atush", den Bewahrer des Waldes.
100 In dieser Region plante der Energieversorger Hydro Quebec Anfang der Siebziger eines der größten Wasserkraftwerke der Welt. Nach hefti-

gem Widerstand der Cree kam es 1975 zu einem Abkommen, dem sich auch die Inuit und die Naskapi anschlossen. Die Selbstverwaltung der 105 Region wurde beschlossen, und auch der Aufbau des Cree Health Boards, dem größten Arbeitgeber der Region. Es gab finanzielle Entschädigungen, und die Landrechte der First Nations wurden anerkannt. 110

[...] Den Cree auf der gegenüberliegenden Seite der James Bay geht es schlechter. Bei ihnen wollte niemand ein Kraftwerk bauen, sie haben keinen so charismatischen Anführer wie Billy Diamond. In ihren Gemeinden sieht man deut- 115 lich die Spätfolgen des „Residential School"-Systems, jener jahrzehntelangen Zwangsumerziehung und des Missbrauchs der First Nations.

[...] Am Abend sind wir in Chisasibi. [...] In der Ferne hören wir ein Brummen. Der 120 „Milkrun" taucht am Himmel auf. Viel zu früh.

Arezu Weitholz, *Frankfurter Allgemeine Zeitung*, 2019

SUPPORT

1. Skim the article and, in English, write down the core message of the text.

_____

_____

2. Find suitable English equivalents for these German words and expressions.

verkehrsblinde Karibus: _____

ungeteerte Schotterpisten: _____

gegen Insektenstiche immun: _____

Pelzjagd: _____

jahrzehntelangen Zwangsumerziehung: _____

3. Read the highlighted phrases in the text and find ways of expressing them in idiomatic English.

Line(s) 3 ff. (*„landen tatsächlich an jeder Milchkanne"*): _____

_____

Line(s) 29 ff. (*„alles ist im Fluss"*): _____

_____

Line(s) 74 ff. (*„dass man sich im Tipi im Uhrzeigersinn bewegt, so wie die Sonne wandert."*): _____

_____

4. Read the text and highlight the essential information using a colour for each aspect: one colour for the description of the region and the countryside and another for Cree culture and customs.

5. Mediate the text writing the script for your oral presentation. Outline the details describing the region and the countryside; then explain what the text says about Cree culture and customs.

10 Global challenges

Behemoth, bully, thief: how the English language is taking over the planet

No language in history has dominated the world quite like English does today.

[...] Behemoth, bully, loudmouth, thief: English is everywhere, and everywhere, English dominates. From inauspicious beginnings on the edge of a minor European archipelago, it has
5 grown to vast size and astonishing influence. Almost 400m people speak it as their first language; a billion more know it as a secondary tongue. It is an official language in at least 59 countries, the unofficial lingua franca of dozens
10 more. No language in history has been used by so many people or spanned a greater portion of the globe. It is aspirational: the golden ticket to the worlds of education and international commerce, a parent's dream and a student's
15 misery, winnower of the haves from the have-nots. It is inescapable: the language of global business, the internet, science, diplomacy, stellar navigation, avian pathology. And everywhere it goes, it leaves behind a trail of
20 dead: dialects crushed, languages forgotten, literatures mangled.

One straightforward way to trace the growing influence of English is in the way its vocabulary has infiltrated so many other
25 languages. For a millennium or more, English was a great importer of words, absorbing vocabulary from Latin, Greek, French, Hindi, Nahuatl and many others. During the 20th century, though, as the US became the dominant
30 superpower and the world grew more connected, English became a net exporter of words. [...]

Yet the influence of English now goes beyond simple lexical borrowing or literary influence. Researchers at the IULM University in
35 Milan have noticed that, in the past 50 years, Italian syntax has shifted towards patterns that mimic English models, for instance in the use of possessives instead of reflexives to indicate body parts and the frequency with which
40 adjectives are placed before nouns. German is also increasingly adopting English grammatical forms, while in Swedish its influence has been changing the rules governing word formation and phonology.
45 Within the anglophone world, that English should be the key to all the world's knowledge and all the world's places is rarely questioned.

The hegemony of English is so natural as to be invisible. Protesting it feels like yelling at the moon. Outside the anglophone world, living 50 with English is like drifting into the proximity of a supermassive black hole, whose gravity warps everything in its reach. Every day English spreads, the world becomes a little more homogenous and a little more bland. 55

Until recently, the story of English was broadly similar to that of other global languages: it spread through a combination of conquest, trade and colonisation. (Some languages, such as Arabic and Sanskrit, also caught on through 60 their status as sacred tongues.) But then, at some point between the end of the second world war and the start of the new millennium, English made a jump in primacy that no amount of talk about it as a "lingua franca" or "global language" 65 truly captures. It transformed from a dominant language to what the Dutch sociologist Abram de Swaan calls a "hypercentral" one.

De Swaan divides languages into four categories. Lowest on the pyramid are the 70 "peripheral languages", which make up 98% of all languages, but are spoken by less than 10% of mankind. These are largely oral, and rarely have any kind of official status. Next are the "central languages", though a more apt term might be 75 "national languages". These are written, are taught in schools, and each has a territory to call its own: Lithuania for Lithuanian, North and South Korea for Korean, Paraguay for Guarani, and so on. 80

Following these are the 12 "supercentral languages": Arabic, Chinese, English, French, German, Hindi, Japanese, Malay, Portuguese,

Russian, Spanish and Swahili – each of which
85 (except for Swahili) boast 100 million speakers
or more. These are languages you can travel
with. They connect people across nations. They
are commonly spoken as second languages,
often (but not exclusively) as a result of their
90 parent nation's colonial past.

Then, finally, we come to the top of the
pyramid, to the languages that connect the
supercentral ones. There is only one: English,
which De Swaan calls "the hypercentral
95 language that holds the entire world language
system together". The Japanese novelist Minae
Mizumura similarly describes English as a

"universal language". For Mizumura, what
makes it universal is not that it has many native
speakers – Mandarin and Spanish have more – 100
but that it is "used by the greatest number of
non-native speakers in the world". She compares
it to a currency used by more and more people
until its utility hits a critical mass and it
becomes a world currency. The literary critic 105
Jonathan Arac is even more blunt, noting, in a
critique of what he calls "Anglo-Globalism", that
"English in culture, like the dollar in economics,
serves as the medium through which knowledge
may be translated from the local to the global." 110
[...]

Jacob Mikanowski, *The Guardian*, 2018

---

1 behemoth *(n)* a very big object/entity • **3** inauspicious *(adj)* unpromising, unfavourable • **15** winnower *(n)* the thing that makes the difference; *das, was die Spreu vom Weizen trennt; das KO-Kriterium* (to winnow – to separate the wheat from the chaff) • **21** to mangle sth. to ruin sth. • **22** to trace to find, to discover • **33** lexical borrowing *(n)* the adoption of words from another language • **37** to mimic to copy, to imitate • **52** proximity *(n)* the state of being close to sth • **56** bland *(adj)* dull, featureless, boring • **65** primacy *(n)* supremacy, importance • **76** apt *(adj)* appropriate, suitable • **105** utility *(n)* usefulness, value

→ To practise with closed reading comprehension tasks, go to tasks 4–7.

1 COMPREHENSION

a) Describe both the positive and negative aspects of English as a world language.

b) Outline the reasons given in the text why English is a "hypercentral" language (l. 68).

2 ANALYSIS Analyse the stylistic devices the author uses to convince the reader of his position. → S10.2

SUPPORT

a) Summarise the author's position in only one sentence.

_____

_____

b) Fill in the table below. Note down the stylistic devices and explain their effect.

Line(s)	Stylistic device	Example and effect
l. 1	*Enumeration (of negative terms) or asyndeton*	"Behemoth, bully, loudmouth, thief" Effect: *creates suspense and emphasis* _____
ll. 1–3		"English is everywhere, and everywhere, English dominates." Effect: _____
ll. 6–10		"400m people … a billion more … in at least 59 countries … of dozens more" Effect: _____
ll. 10–12		"No language in history has been … or spanned a greater portion of the globe" Effect: _____

Line(s)	Stylistic device	Example and effect
ll. 12–16		"It is aspirational … It is inescapable" Effect: _____
ll. 14–15		"a parent's dream and a student's misery" Effect: _____
ll. 16–18		"the language of global business, the internet, science, diplomacy, … avian pathology." Effect: _____
ll. 19–20		"everywhere it goes, it leaves behind a trail of dead" Effect: _____
ll. 20–21		"dialects crushed, languages forgotten, literatures mangled" Effect: _____

3 EVALUATION Do **one** of the following tasks.

"English is everywhere, and everywhere, English dominates." Comment on this statement with reference to the views expressed in the text and your own experience of the use of English today.

OR

Write a letter to the author in which you comment on his article. State why you liked/did not like it and explain why you found/did not find it convincing. Include a passage in which you outline why English is (not) very important to you personally. → S19.1

TIP

Remember that in order to argue your case in a meaningful way, you have to refer to the text and quote from it. Use a formal style of writing. Make the letter short, to the point and polite, even when criticising the article.

OR

You have been invited to speak at an international youth conference on "The Future of English." Refer to the text you have read and your knowledge gained in class.
Read the tip and write your speech. → S15

TIP

Remember that you will be speaking to a group of peers. Try to attract your listeners' attention at the beginning and use rhetorical devices in order to get your message across clearly and convincingly. Provide examples and give a short summary of your message at the end.

4 MULTIPLE CHOICE Tick the correct answer.

1. The total number of people who speak English either as their first or as a foreign language is …

☐ a) 400 million.   ☐ b) 600 million.   ☐ c) one billion.   ☐ d) 1.4 billion.

2. English is used as an official language in _____ countries.

☐ a) fewer than 59   ☐ b) at least 59   ☐ c) exactly 59   ☐ d) dozens of

5 TRUE OR FALSE Tick the correct box. Give the line number(s) and the first and last three words of the quote from the text to prove your assertions.

	True	False
1. The global spread of the English language contributes to the decay and destruction of other dialects, languages and literatures. Line(s): _____		
2. From its beginnings until today, the English language has always been "a net exporter of words." Line(s): _____		
3. The grammar of the Italian language has heavily influenced English grammar. Line(s): _____		
4. The sound system of the Swedish language has been influenced by English. Line(s): _____		
5. A national language is a language that is used exclusively in only one specific country. Line(s): _____		
6. For touristic purposes, it is advisable and useful to speak a supercentral language. Line(s): _____		

6 SHORT ANSWERS Give short answers. You need not write complete sentences. Explain what the author intends to express by the underlined passages.

1. "Protesting it feels like yelling at the moon." (ll. 49–50)

_____

2. "[…] living with English is like drifting into the proximity of a supermassive black hole […]" (ll. 50–52)

_____

7 RANKING Rank the four terms according to their global linguistic importance and impact. Use the lines to fill in these terms:

central language   hypercentral language   peripheral language   supercentral language

_____

_____

_____

_____

A1 ◁)) **8** MULTIPLE CHOICE Listen to John Vidal, the *Guardian*'s environment editor, discussing the pressure on water, one of the world's most precious resources. He is speaking with Dr Peter Gleick, an expert on water. Tick the correct answer. Only **one** answer is correct.

1. John Vidal begins the interview by posing a question about the availability and quality of water and its impact on development in …

☐ a) Europe and Africa.

☐ b) North and South America.

☐ c) Asia and Australia.

☐ d) all of the above.

2. According to Dr Gleick, whether a person has access to water depends on their …

☐ a) daily water consumption.

☐ b) tax rate or income.

☐ c) place of birth or residence.

☐ d) attitude to water as a resource.

3. The majority of people living in industrialised countries believes that access to water is not …

☐ a) important for survival.

☐ b) a human right.

☐ c) an extraordinary thing.

☐ d) cheap.

4. If people have neither drinkable running water nor usable water toilets, they will …

☐ a) have to move their homes nearer to water sources.

☐ b) have extreme difficulty improving their financial and social status.

☐ c) have to rely on water supplies provided by NGOs.

☐ d) have to pay for clean water.

5. In numerous countries a lot of young women and small children suffer because they often have a long way to walk to the nearest …

☐ a) wells.

☐ b) shops.

☐ c) schools.

☐ d) fields.

9 SHORT ANSWERS Give short answers. You need not write complete sentences.

1. Dr Peter Gleick is the founder of a research facility in the US. What is its name?

_____

2. Political disputes over water are intensifying in several countries. Name them.

_____

3. What is the Water Conflict Chronology?

_____

4. Which groups are involved in violent conflicts over water?

_____

5. How did the United Nations deal with the issue of water …

a) before 2010? _____

b) in 2010? _____

c) What are the consequences? _____

10 MEDIATION Your English class is participating in an Erasmus Plus project entitled "The future of globalisation." Together with a number of other high schools across Europe you have set up a joint website, where each school contributes an article on the topic. Your teacher has asked you to write an article on "The increase and decrease in globalisation since 1989" using the relevant information from the text below.

Nach dem Kahlschlag

Vorbei war die Globalisierung schon vor der Pandemie

Während wir uns nämlich noch mitten im Sturm wähnten, hatte der sich längst gelegt. Dabei ist es weit mehr als nur ein Zeitvertreib, die Bewegungsrichtung der Globalisierung zu bestim-
5 men. In großen Krisen verteilen sich die weltweiten Kräfte wie im Zeitraffer neu, und die Frage ist vor allem, wie die Großen abschneiden: China, die USA und Europa. Und weil auf die Dauer Macht und Einfluss ohne ökonomischen
10 Erfolg versiegen, spielen die weltwirtschaftlichen Verhältnisse für dieses Kräftemessen eine entscheidende Rolle.

Dalia Marin kann genau erklären, wann und warum die Globalisierung haltgemacht hat.
15 „Seit dem Jahr 2011 stagniert der Offenheitsgrad in der Weltwirtschaft", sagt die Professorin für Internationale Wirtschaftsbeziehungen an der TU München. Festmachen lässt sich das unter anderem daran, wie sich der Welthandel und die
20 globale Wirtschaftsleistung entwickeln. Wächst der Handel der Nationen miteinander deutlich schneller als ihre Volkswirtschaften insgesamt, dann nimmt die Offenheit weltweit zu. Die Konzerne verteilen ihre Produktionsstätten weiter
25 rund um den Erdball, es wird mehr grenzüberschreitend investiert.

So war es im letzten Jahrzehnt des alten und im ersten Jahrzehnt des neuen Jahrtausends. „Hyperglobalisierung" nennt Dalia Marin diese
30 Phase, die mit dem Fall der Mauer begann. Auf einmal bot sich Osteuropa für deutsche und westeuropäische Unternehmen als Quelle billiger, aber qualifizierter Arbeit dar – und das nah an den Heimatmärkten. Also begannen die Fa-
35 briken zu wandern. Auch China öffnete sich weiter, im Jahr 2001 trat es der Welthandelsorganisation bei und signalisierte damit: Wir halten uns an die globalen Regeln. Das war der zweite Turbo für die Globalisierung. Mehr und mehr
40 Lieferketten wurden bis Ostasien gestreckt, Vor- und Zwischenprodukte überquerten nationale Grenzen. Deutsche Maschinen gingen nach China, erst kamen Turnschuhe zurück, dann Solarpanels, schließlich Smartphones.
45 Die Globalisierungsparty endete mit der Finanzkrise im Jahr 2008 und dem anschließen-

den Absturz der Weltwirtschaft. Der machte nicht nur manche Menschen ärmer und erschreckte andere, sondern erinnerte auch die Wirtschafts-führer an die Verletzlichkeit ihres
50 Systems. Was, wenn nun auch der Protektionismus wiederkäme? Die Unsicherheit nahm weltweit zu – innerhalb von vier Jahren um 200 Prozent, wie Dalia Marin erklärt.

Woher sie das weiß? Sie schwört auf einen
55 Weltunsicherheitsindex, der die Texte in Wirtschaftszeitungen auf die Kommunikation von Unsicherheit hin auswertet. Je öfter sie zur Sprache kommt, desto prekärer ist die wahrgenommene Lage. Aufgrund der damaligen Verunsi-
60 cherung, so Marin, wurden Lieferketten verkürzt, wurden Produktionen nach Hause geholt und mit vielen Robotern ausgestattet, damit die Arbeitskosten im Rahmen blieben. Auch nach der Krise investierten die Unternehmen
65 wenig, weil die Verbraucher sich nicht so leicht an große Anschaffungen herantrauten. Nachdem der Welthandel vor der Finanzkrise deutlich schneller gewachsen war als die globale Wirtschaftsleistung, entwickelten sich beide
70 nun in etwa gleich. Unter dem Strich bedeutete das im vergangenen Jahrzehnt eine Stagnation.

Die 20 führenden Industrie- und Schwellenländer begannen sich nach der Finanzkrise abzuschotten, schützten ihre Bauern, wehrten sich
75 mit neuen Zöllen gegen angebliche Dumpingpreise der Partner. Der Handel wurde zusehends unfreier. Im Jahr 2016 zählte die Welthandelsorganisation einen neuen Höchststand von 1263 zusätzlichen Schutzmaßnahmen. Da regierte
80 der Protektionist Donald Trump noch gar nicht in Washington. Spätestens mit ihm und seinen Vertrauten hat die Globalisierung vom Vorwärts- in den Rückwärtsgang geschaltet.

In diese Situation ist nun das Coronavirus
85 geplatzt und versetzt der Weltwirtschaft einen entscheidenden Schlag. "Wir erleben gerade einen völlig neuen Grad an Unsicherheit", sagte Amerikas oberster Zentralbanker Jerome Powell vergangene Woche. Dalia Marin findet das be-
90 stätigt: "Unser Modell besagt, dass durch Corona die Unsicherheit um 300 Prozent steigt."

Sie erwartet, dass die Zinsen dank der von den Zentralbanken ausgelösten Geldschwemme
95 noch einmal kräftig sinken werden. Das wiederum würde es Unternehmen noch leichter machen, die sogenannte Deglobalisierung zu finanzieren. Sie können die um den Erdball gezogenen Lieferketten umbauen, Produktionen zurück nach Hause holen und in ihren Fabriken 100 viele Roboter einsetzen, um die Arbeitskosten im Zaum zu halten. Marin rechnet damit, dass Corona die Rückverlagerung um ein Drittel und die Ausstattung mit Robotern sogar um zwei Drittel beschleunigt. 105

Uwe Jean Heuser, *Die Zeit*, 2020

SUPPORT

1. In English, write down the core message of the text.

_____

_____

_____

2. Find suitable English equivalents for the German words and expressions.

l. 6: wie im Zeitraffer: _____

l. 11: Kräftemessen: _____

l. 30: Fall der Mauer: _____

l. 56: Weltunsicherheitsindex: _____

l. 71: unter dem Strich: _____

l. 94: Geldschwemme: _____

3. Find ways of expressing the highlighted phrases in the text in idiomatic English.

ll. 15 ff.: „[…] stagniert der Offenheitsgrad in der Weltwirtschaft'"

_____

ll. 34 ff.: „Also begannen die Fabriken zu wandern."

_____

ll. 38 ff.: „Das war der zweite Turbo für die Globalisierung."

_____

ll. 74 ff:: „[…] begannen sich nach der Finanzkrise abzuschotten"

_____

ll. 83 ff.: „[…] vom Vorwärts- in den Rückwärtsgang geschaltet."

_____

ll. 86 ff.: „[…] versetzt der Weltwirtschaft einen entscheidenden Schlag."

_____

4. Read the text and highlight the relevant information using the following colour coding:
   • reasons for the increase and acceleration of globalisation
   • results of the increase and acceleration of globalisation
   • reasons for the decrease and deceleration of globalisation
   • results of the decrease and deceleration of globalisation

5. Now mediate the text. Pay close attention to the task and use your notes.

11 MONOLOGUE Describe and analyse the bar chart. Use the information to present your NGO to your partner. → **S26.1**

Partner A

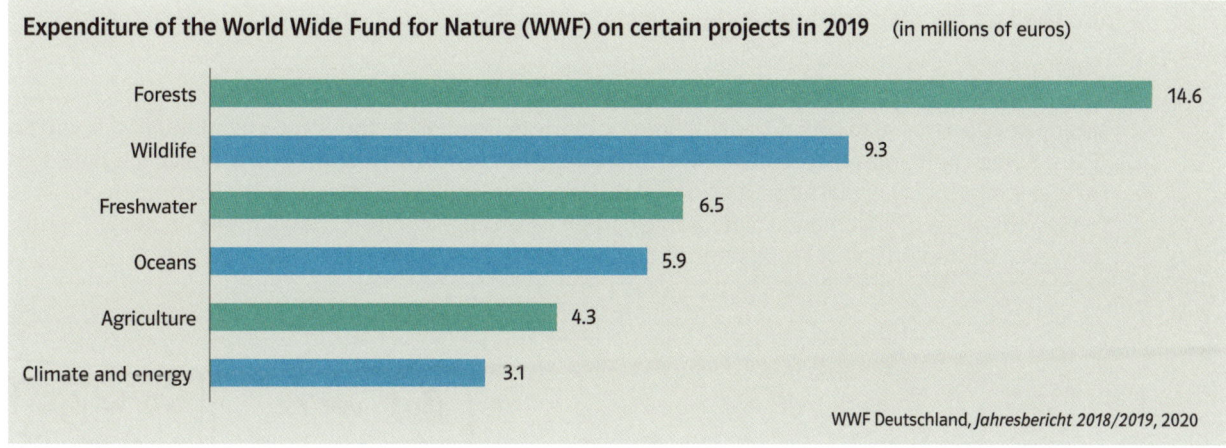

Expenditure of the World Wide Fund for Nature (WWF) on certain projects in 2019 (in millions of euros)

Forests	14.6
Wildlife	9.3
Freshwater	6.5
Oceans	5.9
Agriculture	4.3
Climate and energy	3.1

WWF Deutschland, *Jahresbericht 2018/2019*, 2020

Partner B

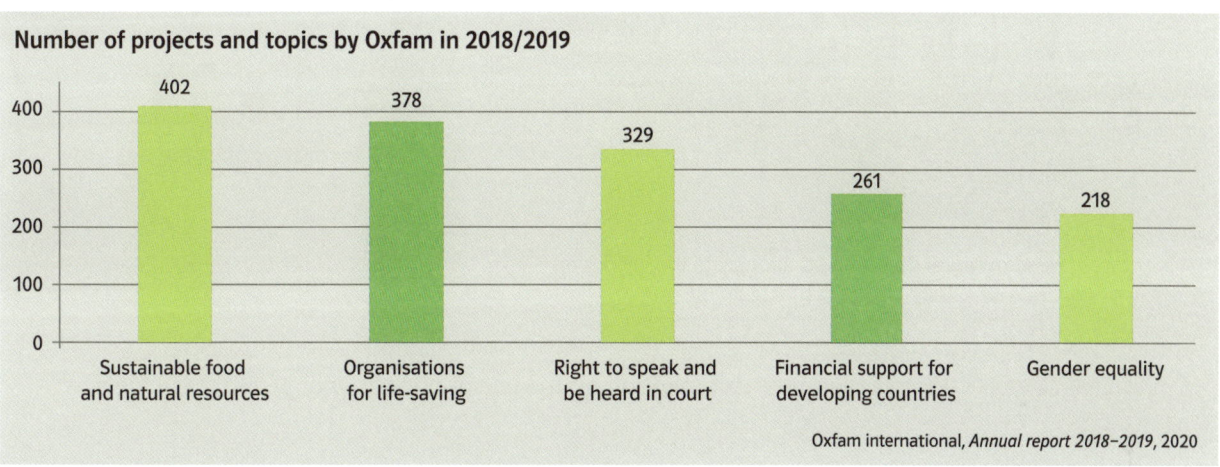

Number of projects and topics by Oxfam in 2018/2019

Sustainable food and natural resources	Organisations for life-saving	Right to speak and be heard in court	Financial support for developing countries	Gender equality
402	378	329	261	218

Oxfam international, *Annual report 2018–2019*, 2020

12 DIALOGUE Together, analyse the bar chart below. Discuss the role, importance and influence of different NGOs on a global scale and why NGOs (do not) contribute to defeating inequality, restoring peace, protecting the environment, etc. Try to agree on your favourite NGO.

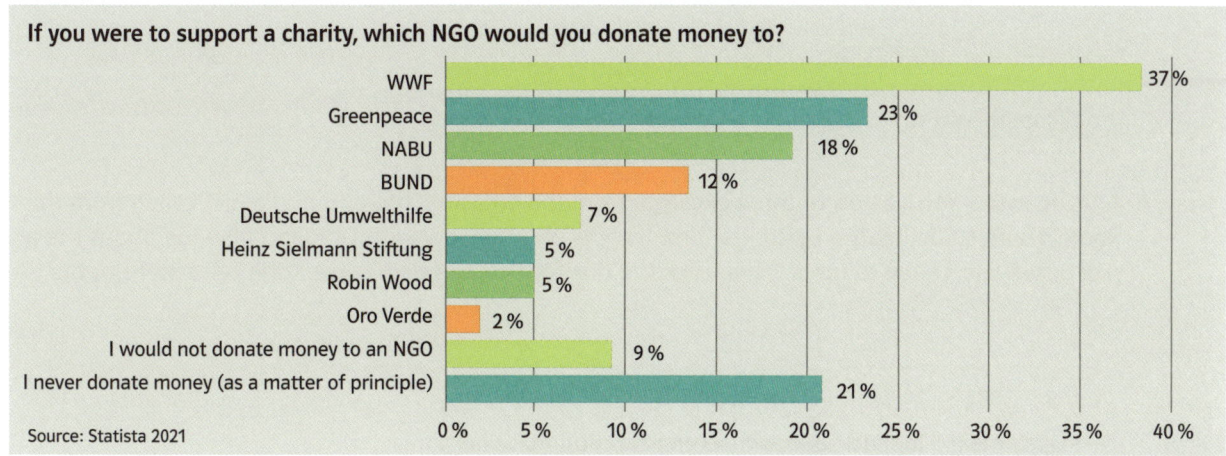

If you were to support a charity, which NGO would you donate money to?

WWF	37 %
Greenpeace	23 %
NABU	18 %
BUND	12 %
Deutsche Umwelthilfe	7 %
Heinz Sielmann Stiftung	5 %
Robin Wood	5 %
Oro Verde	2 %
I would not donate money to an NGO	9 %
I never donate money (as a matter of principle)	21 %

Source: Statista 2021

Our favourite NGO is _____

because _____

11 Ecological challenges

1 VISUALS In pairs, take turns describing and analysing the cartoons. Read the info box first. Use vocabulary from the fact file, your portfolio and the Spot on facts in your coursebook to complete the task.

FACT FILE

Many people choose to offset their carbon footprint to feel better about the environmental impact of their lives. Some companies use carbon offset schemes, often for marketing purposes, which are based on the idea of investing money in planting trees or supporting other environmental projects to compensate for CO_2 emissions caused by human activity. Some carbon offsetting schemes are voluntary. In many countries, however, carbon pricing is an offsetting scheme imposed on industries by law.

"I kind of regret objecting so strongly to the wind farm they originally had planned."

2 CREATIVE TASK Write a blog post commenting on the use of nuclear energy and fossil fuels.

OR

Write a blog post expressing your opinion about offset schemes involving planting trees to compensate for CO2 emissions.

3 BEFORE YOU START Look up these words in a dictionary. Add them to your list of words related to the topic 'ecology' and use it to complete the tasks below. → S3

| domestic … | packaging | bulk | drainage | to drive sth | to convert sth | polymer(s) |

| to tailor sth into sth | disposal | menace | carrier | bags |

A1 ◁)) **4** TRUE OR FALSE You'll listen to three excerpts from the episode "The end of plastic", taken from the BBC Radio 4 series Costing the Earth. The first track is an interview with Dr Julian Allwood about the amount of plastic we use. Listen to track 1, then tick the box for true or false. Correct the false statements. → S21

	True	False
1. The highest amount of plastic waste is produced at home.		
2. Plastic is used for packaging and as constructing material.		
3. Allwood regards plastics as the main reason for an increase in carbon emission.		
4. In his "private research" Allwood found out that the weight of plastic bags used per week was higher than the weight of bottles and cartons.		
5. He regards the use of plastic for industrial purposes as the number one problem.		

5 BEFORE YOU START Before you listen to the second track, write a general definition for the following words:

application: _____

single-use: _____

vital: _____

cross infection: _____

A2 🔊 **6** LISTENING

a) Now listen to track 2, an interview with Philip Law from the British Plastics Federation and his answer to Allwood. Contrast Philip Law's attitude towards the use of plastic to Allwood's point of view. Write on a separate piece of paper.

b) After listening, note down more situations in which the use of plastic is inevitable.

A3 🔊 **7** TABLE COMPLETION Now listen to track 3, the interviews with Emily Smith and Taino Uitto who are trying to live without plastic. Fill in the table for the various stages Emily went through on her way to a plastic-free life.

stage/place	Emily's activities	Emily's feelings/thoughts
in her house, her cupboards		
started off in the bathroom		
emptied her cupboards		
avoided the supermarkets/went to independent stores		

8 SENTENCE COMPLETION Finish the sentences with appropriate information from the interview.

1. The deeper Taino got into the idea of living without plastics …

_____

_____

2. After three years Taino came to the conclusion that …

_____

_____

TIP

Check your room (at home) for things made of plastic. How many items do you find and how many of them could be replaced by alternative materials? Make a list.

12 Science and visions of the future

Echo Boy – a different perspective on mankind

In the following excerpt from the novel *Echo Boy*, which is set in the 22nd century, Daniel does a mind-log (sort of a diary entry for recording his thoughts about his 'birth').

Remember.

The thing burning into my shoulder caused me a significant amount of pain. My arms were strapped tight. I was in some kind of a container.
5 My body was in thick liquid up to my neck. The liquid was rising slowly. It was now touching my chin. At first this was a passive observation, and one made without knowing such words as 'liquid' and 'chin'.

10 But slowly there came instinct.

(This is what I have discovered. Before thought, before knowledge, there is instinct. It is the root of everything.)

And the instinct I had was: Panic.

15 Without understanding why, I felt I had to get out of there. I pulled desperately on the straps. I screamed. The scream was not a word. I did not scream 'Help!' – I would have, if I'd known to do so, but I didn't. The scream was just noise.
20 A desperate roar that gave me enough strength for my arms, then legs, to break free of their constraints.

This is when I started banging on the side of the tank.

25 I kept banging and screaming until I heard something that wasn't a bang or a scream.

The sound was coming from outside. I think there was a sense of relief that there was an outside, and that the whole world wasn't
30 confined to a tank full of ever-rising liquid.

Something was opening the tank. Something, someone – whatever. [...] I fell a short distance onto hard ground. [...]

A noise.

35 Something getting nearer.

Someone.

It was a woman. I know that now, but I didn't know it then. She had long hair and wore white clothes. She was on her own. She came close to
40 me. She knelt beside me. Her face was frowning. She said things, but I think she knew I couldn't understand them.

She had something in her hand. It was small and grey and moving. If I'd ever seen a centipede,
45 I might have thought I was one. Though, of

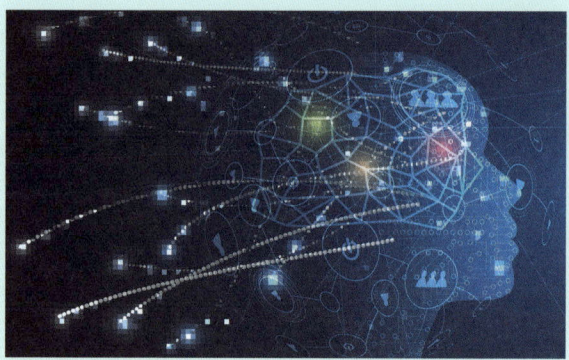

course, it wasn't. It wasn't anything alive. She placed it between her thumb and her finger and mimed putting it in her ear, and then pointed it at me. At my ear.

I understood enough about this instruction to 50 put it to my ear after she had given it me.

Within seconds it was moving in my head. I could feel it inside me. It wasn't painful. It wasn't even weird, because to find something weird you have to have had experience of 55 normality. But I didn't have experience of anything.

Then I must have shut down. That thing inside my head had shut me down. Because there was a gap. A time that I can't remember. 60 A gap during which I was born.

When I woke up, everything was different. I understood things. I understood that I was lying on a bed – futon – on a floor, and I knew that the floor was made from a cloth of ceramic 65 fibres, and I also somehow knew that this particular type of material had been invented in 2067 [...].

On my skin I felt the keratin from the preservation fluid that had covered me in 70 the tank.

I sat up. I looked around. I was somewhere else. I was in a house. A villa. In the desert. There was a photographic poster on the wall of a skyline and the words NEW NEW York. (New 75 New York – human population: 17,345,952; Echo population: 5,492,600.) Also there was a cross on the wall with a small sculpture of a dying man fastened to it. I had no knowledge about this

80 man, except that he was made of pewter. The room's size was easy for me to measure. Indeed, it happened automatically. Six by four metres.

There was the distant sound of a man coughing.

85 And there was the woman. She was standing above me and looking down. I understood that she was thirty-eight years old and that she was free from unnatural genetic or surgical enhancement. Her face was handsome, which 90 was a word normally used for men, but it fitted her more than beautiful. [...]

She spoke to me.

She said: *"Hola. Me llamo Rosella."* [...]

Later she would tell me that the bug-like 95 thing that had got inside my head was called an igniter. It basically switched on my knowledge.

The knowledge that had been programmed into me. I was programmed to know all kinds of things. I knew that I was on a water planet called Earth that had travelled through space at 100 107,279 kilometres an hour. I knew that the universe we belonged to was a million million million million kilometres across. I knew the composition of the air, and could tell, just by inhaling, how much was nitrogen and how much 105 was oxygen. [...]

I knew that I was an Echo, and that an Echo's function was to serve humans, without question. [...]

"Y tú te llamas Daniel." 110

I heard my name and found it weird that I knew so much, and yet had to be told what my name was.

Matt Haig, *Echo Boy*, 2014

Echo short for 'Enhanced Computerised Humanoid Organism' • **4 to strap** to fasten with a strap, i.e. a long strip of leather or similar material • **22 constraint** sth that limits or restricts your freedom • **44 centipede** small wormlike animal with many legs • **69 keratin** protein material making up hair, nails and the outer layer of human skin • **80 pewter** *Zinn*

→ To practise with closed reading comprehension tasks, go to tasks 4 – 6.

1 COMPREHENSION Describe how Daniel comes into being.

2 ANALYSIS Analyse how Daniel's birth is portrayed. Focus on the process, choice of words and sentence structure.

3 EVALUATION Daniel is an Echo who is to serve humans unconditionally. To what extent is this type of creation beneficial to mankind? Comment on this question.

4 TRUE OR FALSE Read the following statements and decide whether they are true or false. Tick the correct box and give reference from the text to support your decision.

	True	False
1. Daniel's actions inside the tank are guided by awareness. Line(s): _____		
2. After falling to the ground, he is helpless. Line(s): _____		
3. The woman in white instructs him how to put the small grey moving object into his ear. Line(s): _____		
4. It feels strange to Daniel when this object moves in his head. Line(s): _____		
5. When Daniel wakes up after his shutdown, he is able to fully take in his surroundings. Line(s): _____		
6. Rosella and Daniel are of the same kind. Line(s): _____		

5 MULTIPLE CHOICE Tick the one right answer.

1. Daniel's 'birth' is started by …

☐ a) shock.

☐ b) surprise.

☐ c) indifference.

☐ d) alarm.

2. In order to be able to leave the tank Daniel …

☐ a) has to be rational.

☐ b) screams "Help".

☐ c) makes a lot of noise.

☐ d) collects his strength and breaks it.

3. The woman in white …

☐ a) holds Daniel in her arms.

☐ b) holds a technical device between her fingers.

☐ c) holds a wormlike animal between her fingers.

☐ d) holds something alive in her hand.

4. When Daniel wakes up after his shut down, …

☐ a) he is in a room in New New York.

☐ b) he is in a big house in the desert.

☐ c) he is in a villa in New New York.

☐ d) he is lying on the floor.

5. Now Daniel …

☐ a) can read and write.

☐ b) knows his name.

☐ c) can understand Spanish.

☐ d) can read people's minds.

6 SHORT ANSWERS Answer the questions.

1. What is the ratio between the human population and the Echo population in New New York?

_____

_____

_____

2. Who is the dying man on the cross that Daniel sees when he wakes up again?

_____

_____

_____

3. Daniel knows that Rosella is thirty-eight years old. What else does he know about her?

_____

_____

_____

4. How has Daniel gathered his knowledge?

_____

_____

_____

_____

7 BEFORE YOU START You are going to listen to a document that focuses on the opportunities and challenges posed by synthetic DNA. The DNA carries the genetic code which contains the instructions for constructing and operating an organism.

Match the words on the left to the expressions on the right.

1 to make to order	☐ A	to put together
2 lab	☐ B	to customise
3 to synthesise	☐ C	a very dangerous disease that was eradicated around 1980
4 to assemble	☐ D	laboratory
5 to pipette	☐ E	to form by combining parts
6 smallpox	☐ F	to transfer or measure liquids in small amounts (e.g. drops)

A1 ◁)) **8** MULTIPLE CHOICE Read the following task before you listen to the report. Tick the one correct answer.

1. The announcer gives examples of the power of genes. She says they are responsible for …

☐ a) making penicillin and growing hair.   ☐ c) growing hair and making insulin.

☐ b) biological instructions and cells.   ☐ d) cells and stuff.

2. How many genes does the scientist interviewed synthesize every month?

☐ a) thousands   ☐ c) 6

☐ b) more than 10,000   ☐ d) around 10,000

3. Designer DNA is inserted into cells to find …

☐ a) bacteria.   ☐ c) a new type of food.

☐ b) a new chemical for drugs.   ☐ d) new substances for medicine or food.

4. Over the last decade the cost of making a designer DNA has dropped …

☐ a) by 90 cents.   ☐ c) by more than 90 per cent.

☐ b) by one tenth.   ☐ d) by 100 per cent.

5. To order DNA …

☐ a) you have to prove that you are a scientist.   ☐ c) you do not need to fulfil any requirements.

☐ b) you need to understand biology.   ☐ d) you have to work for a pharmaceutical firm.

9 SENTENCE COMPLETION Fill in the missing information.

1. At Twist Bioscience orders go through a security screening to …

_____

2. A key biosecurity issue is …

_____

3. Another challenge is posed by new desktop synthesizers. They …

_____

4. To respond to this challenge the biosecurity expert Gigi Gronvall suggests that …

_____

5. After all, officials of the Department of Health and Human Services …

_____

10 MEDIATION Examine the task. A mediation task can be quite complex. Before you start to write your text, plan it carefully. First, single out the different elements of the task, such as:

- the addressee of your text,
- the format of your target text,
- the focus of your text,
- the purpose of your text.

TIP

Use different colours to help you visualise these various elements.

Determine these elements for the following text.
Your school participates in an eTwinning project with a partner school in Finland. The topic of your project is "Visions of Our Future – Utopia or Dystopia?" Your task is to present scenarios of alternative worlds in a video conference to your eTwinning partners and discuss these scenarios. While doing your research, you have come across this extract which you find highly suitable for your presentation. Write the script for your presentation, focusing on the characteristics of the world as presented in this extract.

11 COMPREHENSION First read the text for the gist. Then scan the text for the relevant information by taking your findings from task 10 into account. Underline those passages.

„Hundert Augen": Überwachen und kuscheln

Die argentinische Autorin schreibt Geschichten wie unbehagliche Träume. In ihrem aktuellen Roman geht es um ferngesteuerte Plüschtiere.

Neuerdings verschenkt Samanta Schweblin gern altes Miniaturspielzeug. Auf ihrem Instagram-Account hat die argentinische Autorin, die seit einigen Jahren in Berlin lebt, das Foto eines win-
5 zigen Plüschvogels geteilt. Sie finde die Tierchen auf Flohmärkten, schreibt Schweblin, wenn man sie danach fragt, und sie kämen ihr vor wie Glücksbringer aus vergangenen Zeiten.

Nun wird es Menschen geben, die den
10 Anblick dieses abgewetzten Kuscheltiers schlicht unschuldig und hübsch finden. Aber auch Menschen, die sofort an Überwachung oder Terror denken, weil sie „Hundert Augen" gelesen haben, so heißt Schweblins neuer
15 Roman.

In ihm geht es um eine Gesellschaft im Bann einer simplen, aber perfiden Erfindung: nämlich um Plüschtiere mit integrierten Kameras, um Pandas, Häschen und Eulen mit elektronischen
20 Eingeweiden, durch deren Augen ein Mensch irgendwo auf dem Planeten den Tierbesitzer beobachten, sogar mit ihm interagieren kann, im Einverständnis beider Teilnehmer.

Die Spielzeuge, genannt Kentukis, bewegen
25 sich – gesteuert vom Menschen auf der anderen Seite der Verbindung – auf rudimentären Rollen und können schnurren, quieken und kreischen, nicht aber sprechen. Wollen die Besitzer mit ihren Kentukis reden, müssen sie sich auf
30 Morsezeichen oder andere Tricks verständigen.

Mit wem man diese Schicksalsgemeinschaft eingeht; ob hinter dem Bildschirm ein Kind oder ein Sexualstraftäter sitzt, kann man sich beim Kauf eines Kentukis nicht aussuchen. Der Zufall
35 entscheidet, und pro Tier wird nur eine Verbindung verkauft. Kappt einer von beiden die Verbindung, ist der Kentuki tot. Das Verblüffende: Nach 252 Seiten versteht man sehr genau, warum Menschen ihre Privatsphäre aufgeben, um
40 sich auf dieses schräge Spiel einzulassen. [...]

In „Hundert Augen" erzählt sie von Menschen, die sich Kentukis als Alltagsbegleiter halten, und Menschen, die zu Kentukis werden. Manche wollen der Enge ihres Alltags entkom-
45 men oder sich nicht mehr allein fühlen, andere sind Voyeure oder Sadisten. Da ist die Pensionärin Emilia aus Peru, die in Gestalt eines Kaninchens zu ihrer jungen Kentuki-Herrin ein fast mütterliches Verhältnis entwickelt.

50 Der Halbwaise Marvin aus Guatemala wird zum Drachen, der sich im norwegischen Honningsvåg auf die Suche nach Schnee begibt, dabei aber die Lust an seinem Offline-Leben verliert. „In drei Wochen würde es die Noten geben,
55 und sie würden grauenhaft ausfallen", heißt es im Buch, „aber gerade war Marvin kein Junge mehr, der einen Drachen besaß, sondern ein Drache, der einen Jungen in sich trug."

In Italien findet der alleinerziehende Vater
60 Enzo in seinem Kentuki, den er rührend höflich mit „Mister" anspricht, einen treuen Unterstützer im Haushalt, während Alina im mexikanischen Oaxaca all ihre Frustration an einer Plüschkrähe auslässt: Weil sie sich in der Künst-
65 lerresidenz, in die sie ihren Freund begleitet, ihrer Durchschnittlichkeit bewusst wird, ver-

stümmelt sie ihren Kentuki – bis er so defizitär aussieht, wie sie sich fühlt. [...]

Samanta Schweblin sagt, sie habe „Hundert
70 Augen" geschrieben, um ihre Technik-Ängste zu untersuchen. „Wir sind alle sehr alert, wenn es um die Orwell'schen Idee einer mächtigen Kontrollinstanz geht, ein Staat oder eine Firma, die über unsere Privatsphäre verfügt", sagt sie. Heu-
75 te ist die „Big Brother"-Erzählung schal geworden: Spätestens seit Edward Snowdens NSA-Enthüllungen muss man sich haarsträubende Spionage-Szenarien gar nicht mehr ausdenken.

Gleichzeitig findet man sich mit Überwachungsparanoia schnell in unangenehmer 80 Gesellschaft wieder. „Die Idee einer Kontrollinstanz ist zwar keine Vorstellung, der ich mich komplett versperre", sagt Schweblin. In ihrem Roman wollte sie aber vor allem über individuelle Verantwortung nachdenken: An welchem 85 Punkt verwandeln sich uninformierte Internet-User – in einer Gesellschaft, die ihrer immer selbstverständlicheren Techniknutzung kaum soziale, gesetzliche und moralische Normen auferlegt – in eine ernste Gefahr? [...] 90

Julia Lorenz, taz website, 2020

---

72 George Orwell is the author of *1984*, a dystopian novel which centres around the idea of mass surveillance and totalitarianism. The key phrase "Big Brother is watching you" refers to the head of state constantly watching its population for control and suppression.
76 Edward Snowden is an American whistle-blower who in 2013 revealed highly classified information about the American National Security Agency's (NSA) activities, thus stimulating discussions on national security and individual privacy.

12 LANGUAGE

a) When you mediate a text, you do not translate it word for word. Instead you convey the main ideas. It helps to have synonyms or paraphrases ready for the more difficult words or phrases in your text. Test your skills and find English equivalents for the following words and expressions in the article:

Example:

perfide Erfindung

perfide: *hinterhältig, gemein, boshaft*

in English: devious, mean, malicious

Erfindung: *Schöpfung*

in English: invention, creation

Then combine an adjective and a noun which convey the idea well: e. g. malicious creation.
Now you try it with:

abgewetztes Kuscheltier   rudimentäre Rollen   Schicksalsgemeinschaft

ein Drache, der einen Jungen in sich trug

b) Look closely at the addressee and the format of your target text to determine the kind of language you should use. Is it formal or informal? Is it the kind of informal language that two good friends would use with one another, or is it more like a teacher might use in front of a class? What kind of background (information) does your addressee have? What contexts need to be explained? It may be difficult to anticipate where your addressee might need additional information. For example, how would you explain *Abistreich* or *Bufdi* in English? Scan the text and decide whether any typical German concepts are used and need to be explained.

13 MEDIATION First set the scene. Briefly include information about the addressee, the occasion, the type of text format you are mediating and the source of your information. The German title may also need to be mediated. For book titles, check whether there is an authorised version in the target language.

Hello to …   I'm … The task of our project is …   For my presentation I've chosen the article "…" written by

… and taken from …   The title amounts to … in English.   The article focuses on the idea of …

14 **BEFORE YOU START** GM food is a controversial topic. With a partner, you will discuss its implications. Read the fact file for background information. Then decide who is A and who is B. → S27

FACT FILE

Genetically engineered or genetically modified (GM) foods have had foreign or altered genes inserted into their genetic codes. Genetic engineering speeds up the age-old process of selective breeding by moving desired genes from one plant into another – or even from an animal to a plant or vice versa.

---

15 **MONOLOGUE** Together with a partner, you will discuss the advantages and disadvantages of GM food. Use the given roles, visuals and information

Partner A
You are an opponent of GM food. To illustrate your view, you have chosen a cartoon and an excerpt from a web article. Describe the cartoon to your partner, sum up the main ideas of the excerpt and relate them to the cartoon's message wherever possible.

Part A

Part B

What's the problem with GM food?

One major problem is the fact that a crop can become the intellectual property of a private company. Traditionally, farmers save some of the seeds from their current crop to plant for next year's harvest.

But when a company owns the rights to a GM crop, they can (and do) forbid farmers from doing this, forcing them to purchase new seed from the patent owners every year. Even if a farmer doesn't grow GM crops, they can blow in from neighbouring fields, making it necessary to purchase a licence for them – or face heavy fines. GM critics say that this gives large corporations too much control over agriculture and the power to exploit farmers.

There also remain a handful of scientists who still have concerns about 'unknown' long-term implications. Anti-GM cellular biologist Dr David Williams says that a genome is not a static environment and claims "inserted genes can be transformed by several different means [which] can happen generations later".

Stevie Shephard, BBC goodfood website, 2019

Partner B

You are a proponent of GM food. To illustrate your view, you have chosen a cartoon and an excerpt from a web article. Describe the cartoon to your partner and relate its message to the main ideas of the excerpt.

Part A

"We would like to be genetically modified to taste like Brussels sprouts."

———————
Brussels sprouts small round green vegetable with a (slightly) bitter taste

Part B

Block on GM rice 'has cost millions of lives and led to child blindness'

Stifling international regulations have been blamed for delaying the approval of a food that could have helped save millions of lives this century. The claim is made in a new investigation of the controversy surrounding the development of Golden Rice by a team of international scientists.

Golden Rice is a form of normal white rice that has been genetically modified to provide Vitamin A to counter blindness and other diseases in children in the developing world. It was developed two decades ago but is still struggling to gain approval in most nations. "Golden Rice has not been made available to those for whom it was intended in the 20 years since it was created," states the science writer Ed Regis. "Had it been allowed to grow in these nations, millions of lives would not have been lost to malnutrition, and millions of children would not have gone blind."

Robin McKie, *The Guardian* online, 2019

16 DIALOGUE On the basis of your information and your knowledge gained in class and beyond, discuss the future of GM food.

13 Shakespeare

If Shakespeare was writing today, he'd be a crime writer

The bestselling author of the Roy Grace mysteries explains how, when he is planning a new villain, the Bard's murderous, manipulative creations are his primary inspiration.

5 **A** William Shakespeare's fascination with the dark side of human nature has always had a big influence on me, ever since my student years when I first began to get to know his works. He created some of the most enduring monsters 10 in literature and today, whenever I am planning a villain for a new novel, I am invariably drawn – as I know are countless of my fellow crime writers – to his plays. His vast canon of vivid, rounded, intensely human personifications of 15 evil are driven by greed, lust, prejudice, sometimes plain sadism. Just as villains are today.

B King Lear provides us with the eye-gouging monster Cornwall, the opportunist Edmund, and 20 the tragic king's hard-arsed daughters, Goneril and Regan (and although we feel pity for Lear himself, he's not exactly Mr Nice Guy, either). Nor is Richard II (murdering his uncle) or Richard III (committing infanticide on his 25 nephews). Hamlet gave us Claudius, the stepfather from hell; while Othello's Iago, with his ferocious intellect and charisma, is a kind of Elizabethan Hannibal Lecter. The name of the wickedly manipulative Lady Macbeth has 30 become synonymous with female evil. Shakespeare's bloodiest play of all, Titus Andronicus, has the Elizabethan Bonnie and Clydes, Tamora and Aron – only they're somehow even nastier.

35 **C** In many ways, though, Shakespeare's scariest monster of all is Shylock in The Merchant of Venice, because he so very human. I was co-producer of the 2004 film, with Al Pacino playing the villain. I know of no other courtroom drama that is so gripping. Antonio, having defaulted on 40 his debt to the despised Jewish moneylender, is fighting for his life. Shylock, driven by long, deep-rooted hatred of him, insists on his right to cut his pound of flesh from the man's body. So powerful is the writing that every time I read 45 or see it, I'm left with white knuckles, convinced that this time Shylock is going to do it! The play is, as we say so often of great thrillers, unputdownable, a complete page-turner.

D The early dramatists knew a thing or two 50 about page-turners – or at least, writing hooks. The five-act structure came out of necessity – with rowdy audiences tending to drink heavily, needing regular "comfort" breaks, and the cast members, often having to shout to be heard, 55 needing a rest. The writers had to ensure the audience came back after each break, just as three centuries later, when the likes of Charles Dickens, Alexandre Dumas and Sir Arthur Conan Doyle were writing serialised fiction and 60 had to end on a cliffhanger each time, to bring back readers to the next week's issue.

E Back in Shakespeare's time if you were a writer, and wanted to reach as many people as possible, plays were the only option. During his 65 lifetime, two-thirds of the population were illiterate – and for those who could read there were few books that were accessible. Although novels, such as Cervantes's Don Quixote, were published during Shakespeare's lifetime, it was 70 not really until the Victorian era that reading became commonplace. And it was not until

1935, when Allen Lane began publishing the first Penguin paperbacks, that quality books
75 finally became affordable to the masses.

F The 18th and 19th centuries saw a steady fall in the number of playwrights and instead, a rise in numbers of novelists. I believe if Shakespeare were writing today, with his genius for
80 characters and his skill at plotting, he would be writing novels – maybe some television miniseries and the occasional movie script. All of these have a far bigger potential "reach" today than plays. With more than 50% of all his plays
85 having a courtroom scene or murder, I believe many of his books would land on the crime shelves of WH Smith and other booksellers across the UK and the globe – alongside, if they were writing now, the latest crime fiction from
90 Dickens, Dostoevsky and Sophocles. [...]

G Recently the Crime Writers' Association sent out a questionnaire asking its members what they thought Shakespeare would be writing today. Author Sarah Hilary, who won the Theakstons Old Peculier crime novel of the year 95 award in 2015, said Shakespeare would specialise in psychological thrillers – seasoned with some delicious political satire. Novelist Julia Crouch called Hamlet "the first great psychological thriller". Author of the Frances 100 Doughty mysteries, Linda Stratmann concurred: "Shakespeare really understood human nature, especially its darker side – he wrote about love and hate, jealousy and greed, injured pride and revenge, all the themes that lead to crime. 105 When we watch a Shakespeare play we recognise ourselves."

Peter James, *The Guardian*, 2016

3 the Bard a name used to refer to Shakespeare • **24 infanticide** killing a child • **28 Hannibal Lecter** a serial killer in the novel and film *The Silence of the Lambs* • **32 Bonnie and Clyde** a pair of robbers in the US in a 1930s road movie • **51 writing hook** a word or idea designed to keep the reader interested • **58 Charles Dickens** (1812–1870) British novelist • **59 Alexandre Dumas** (1824–1895) French author, including *The Three Musketeers* • **59 Sir Arthur Conan Doyle** (1859–1930) author of the Sherlock Holmes stories • **74 Penguin** British publishing company • **87 WH Smith** a British company with shops selling books, newspapers, stationery etc. • **90 Fyodor Dostoevsky** (1821–1881) Russian author • **90 Sophocles** (496–406 BC) ancient Greek author of tragic drama

→ To practise with closed reading comprehension tasks, go to tasks 4–5.

1 COMPREHENSION Outline the writer's reasons for claiming that Shakespeare would be a crime writer in the modern world.

2 ANALYSIS
Analyse the means the author uses to show his fascination with Shakespeare as a crime writer.

USEFUL PHRASES

Connecting words
to begin with • moreover • furthermore • additionally • in addition to • apart from • besides • as well as

SUPPORT

Stylistic means
You want to find out how the author uses language in order to show his fascination. So first check that you understand what these stylistic means and other style decisions are and what effect they might create. Then look for examples in the text and fill in the table as preparation for your answer.

repetition • enumeration • choice of words • register • literary terms • expert quotes

Means (and definition)	Examples from the text	Line refs	Effect

3 EVALUATION "Shakespeare really understood human nature … When we watch a Shakespeare play we recognise ourselves." (ll. 102–107) Discuss this quote, giving examples from Shakespeare plays you know.
OR
Write a letter or an email to the editor of *The Guardian*, discussing to what extent Shakespeare can be called a crime writer.

USEFUL PHRASES

Talking about crime fiction
to create/focus on suspense • suspenseful, full of intrigue • to track down criminals • to focus on a crime • to reveal the villain (early in the story) • an unknown criminal/villain • to circle the theme of good vs. evil • to break the law • wrong deeds must be avenged • justice must be restored • to be involved in/to commit a crime • to crack/solve the case • detective • to use one's powers of deduction • a trail of suspects • a race against time • fast-paced • to solve a puzzle/the mystery, to leave a story unresolved

---

TIP

Writing a letter to the editor
Purpose: Offering comment, agreement or disagreement or giving additional information
Preparation: List the author's arguments and write your opinion next to them; decide on the purpose of the letter (support, criticism, etc.)
Writing:
• Follow the rules of a formal letter (neutral to formal register, no colloquial language)
• For the salutation, use "Sir/Madam" (without "Dear")
• Do not address the editor and omit the closing lines
• End your letter with your real name and place of residence (town/city name)
Introduction: State which article you are referring to and state your purpose
Main part: Put forward your arguments including a personal perspective or experience
Ending: Write convincing concluding sentences

4 SEQUENCING Read the text and match the statements 1–8 with the paragraphs A–G. There is one more statement than you need.

1 The author claims that nowadays, Shakespeare's genre would be crime fiction.
2 Writers in the past were using unresolved stopping points in order to create suspense.
3 The author of this text models his cruel characters on Shakespeare's evildoers.
4 According to the author, The Merchant of Venice is Shakespeare's most enthralling play.
5 Shakespeare has always been a role model for other playwrights.
6 Contemporary crime writers assume that Shakespeare would write psychological thrillers if he lived today.
7 As reading was not as common in the Elizabethan era, writers had to think of alternative ways to find their audiences.
8 Shakespeare's villains have their equivalents in contemporary literature and film.

Paragraph	A	B	C	D	E	F	G
Statement no.							

5 TRUE OR FALSE Decide if the following statements are true or false and tick the correct box. Give the line number(s) and the first and last three words of the quote from the text to prove your assertions.

	True	False	Line refs.
1. Shakespeare's writing has inspired many modern writers.			
2. The author explicitly names eight plays by Shakespeare.			
3. According to the author, *The Merchant of Venice* is the most riveting courtroom drama.			
4. The list of Shakespearean villains includes Hamlet.			
5. Plays in Shakespeare's time needed several intervals.			
6. In the 19th century, reading books became customary.			
7. Unlike Dickens' and Dostoevsky's novels, Shakespeare's books would be found in the crime section of bookshops.			
8. Only female writers responded to the Crime Writers Association's questionnaire.			

A1 ◁)) **6** SEQUENCING In this BBC programme Matthew Parris talks with Daisy Goodwin (TV producer) and Dominic Dromgoole (artistic director of the Globe Theatre) about Shakespeare and his work. Listen to the talk, then identify the right headlines and put them into the correct order. There are four more headlines than you need.

A Audiences keen on theatre performances	F Rebuilding the Globe
B Special features of the Globe Theatre	G Brilliant female roles
C Movies about Shakespeare	H Constantly improving texts
D Shakespeare today – writing for the TV	I No women allowed on stage
E Shakespeare as an actor and theatre company director	J Shakespeare the feminist
	K Elizabethan dress codes

Order of appearance	1	2	3	4	5	6	7
Letter							

7 SHORT ANSWERS Listen to the talk again. Give short answers in key words or phrases.

1. Which features make the Globe Theatre so special? (Give three examples.)

_____

_____

2. Why is the space behind one of the doors onto the stage in the Globe Theatre a very "Shakespearean place"? (Give two examples.)

_____

_____

3. What are the similarities between writing for a soap opera crew and for an Elizabethan theatre company? (Give two examples.)

_____

_____

8 MEDIATION An international theatre blog offering ideas for youth theatre companies is looking for contributions on innovative ways to play Shakespeare in difficult times, when only a few members of the theatre troupe are available. You have come across this article. Write a blog entry outlining how this theatre company adapted their performance of Macbeth to compensate for difficult conditions.

Theater in Dresden: Fragmente der Trauer

Eigentlich liegt über diesem Stück ein Fluch. Eine Legende besagt, dass 1606, bei einer der ersten Aufführungen von Macbeth, in Shakespeares legendärem Globe Theatre, ein Schau-
5 spieler, der Lady Macbeth verkörpern sollte, an plötzlichem Fieber starb. Shakespeare selbst musste angeblich einspringen, um den Theaterabend zu retten. Im 18. Jahrhundert kam es zu mehreren Aufführungen, bei denen der Bühnen-
10 dolch durch ein echtes Schwert ausgetauscht wurde, was in blutigen Morden endete. Und in der Theaterwelt gilt es bis heute als unglückbringendes Sakrileg, den Namen des Stücks auszusprechen.
15   Das Dresdner Schauspielhaus hat sich davon nicht abbringen lassen und eine Neuinszenierung von Macbeth bei dem Sänger und Schauspieler Christian Friedel in Auftrag gegeben. Doch auch diese Produktion stand bisher unter
20 keinem guten Stern. Die Premiere, die im März stattfinden sollte, musste wegen der Pandemie abgesagt werden, die Uraufführung ist auf Januar 2021 verschoben. Damit das Publikum trotzdem schon zu Beginn der Spielzeit ein bisschen
25 Macbeth-Luft schnuppert, haben Friedel und seine Band „Woods of Birnam" einen theatralischen Konzertabend konzipiert, der „Essenzen" präsentieren und den Zuschauern einen live aufgeführten „Trailer" von dem zeigen soll, was
30 kommen wird. Eine unübliche, aber keineswegs abwegige Idee. Gebannt wartet das Publikum auf die erste Szene, aber der Anfang der „Essenz" ist ein wirklicher Videotrailer, der die aufwendigen Proben für das Stück, die Probleme während
35 der Pandemie und die allgegenwärtige Frage, was das Theater in diesen Zeiten ausrichten kann, beantworten soll. Plötzlich, nachdem Christian Friedel den nicht auszusprechenden Namen seiner Hauptrolle im Video ausgespro-
40 chen hat, bricht der Film ab. In der Dunkelheit herrscht Stille, bis das grelle Licht im Saal aufleuchtet und ein vehementer Hochfrequenzschrei ertönt. Auf der Bühne werden bei dieser Aufführung nur zwei Charaktere zu sehen sein, Macbeth selbst und seine Gemahlin Lady 45
Macbeth.
    Friedel verkörpert einen getriebenen Macbeth, verzweifelt, einsam und voller toxischer Selbstzweifel. Sein Gesicht ist bleich. Der stattliche Körper ist stets gebeugt, die Schultern 50
hängen herab, als wären sie ihm fremd. Eindringlich sind besonders die Szenen, die die fiebrigen Träume des jungen Königs illustrieren. Antagonistisch und symbiotisch zugleich gibt sich Lady Macbeth, die von Nadja Stübiger gespielt 55
wird. Sie ist eine hartherzige Gattin, berechnend, aber auch voller Liebe. Doch ihr Ehrgeiz und ihre Gier nach Macht sorgen dafür, dass sie Macbeths Männlichkeit in Frage stellt und ihn zum Mord an Duncan treibt. Friedel hat einen düsteren 60
Macbeth konzipiert, mit einer Hauptfigur, die zwischen Depression und Wollust, Gier und Antriebslosigkeit hin und her schwankt. Videos zeigen die dunkle Magie der drei Hexen im Birnam Forest, sie stellen den anschwellenden Wahn- 65
sinn des Königs dar, der wie von Sinnen seinen Kopf mit erratischem Blick bewegt und hinter dem wie ein Omen die Königskrone aufblitzt.
    Aber nicht nur das Schauspiel, auch die Musik interpretiert das traditionsreiche Shakes- 70
peare-Stück neu. „Woods of Birnam", Friedels Band, die nach dem Birnam Forest aus Macbeth benannt ist und 2011 von Friedel und vier anderen Musikern gegründet wurde, hat sich ganz der Vertonung von Theatertexten gewidmet und 75
generiert mit ihren Indieballaden, basierend auf den Texten des englischen Autors, atmosphärische Klangräume, die mit dem minimalistischen Bühnenbild eine träumerische Verbindung eingehen. [...] 80

Kevin Hanschke, *Frankfurter Allgemeine Zeitung*, 2020

USEFUL PHRASES

Talking about the theatre
to play the lead role • to film the performance on video • to produce • to direct • to rehearse scenes • on the opening night • how the audience might react to … • to portray (a character) as … • to offer a new/imaginative/quirky/eccentric interpretation of … • when the curtain rises/falls, the audience sees …

9 MONOLOGUE

Partner A

1. Describe your cartoon. Then explain how the cartoonist aims to combine Shakespeare's literary work with life today.

2. Hamlet's famous monologue: Describe the second cartoon. A cartoonist often aims at criticising an aspect of contemporary times. Explain what the criticism in this cartoon might be and what the connection to *Hamlet* is.

"Oh. Wow. Another sonnet."

Partner B

1. Describe your cartoon. Then explain how the cartoonist aims to combine Shakespeare's literary work with life today.

2. Hamlet's famous monologue: Describe the second cartoon. Explain the point the cartoonist wants to make.

"Compare me to a summer's day? In this country?!"

"He's like, 'To be or not to be,' and I'm, like, 'Get a life.'"

👥 **10** DIALOGUE → S23

a) Discuss how appealing each of these theatre posters and each play's short summary are to you, giving reasons. Agree on which of the posters is more effective.

b) Agree on which of the two plays you would both prefer to go and watch in the theatre.

Two teens fall in love, and consequently six people die.

There's no problem that can't be solved with vague magic.

Abi revision

Basics

Use these pages to check and improve your writing, language and speaking skills before exams.

Before writing – revising your language skills

1 SHORT AND LONG FORMS

a) Start your revision with something easy: In most writing tasks (i.e. all formal texts – not for informal letters/emails or tabloid articles), you should use long forms. Fill in the long forms here.

1. isn't	2. won't	3. I'm	4. haven't	5. she's/he's	6. it's	7. they're	8. you'll
				she/he is **OR** *she/he has*	**OR**		

TIP

"have" vs. "have got"
- In formal English (written and spoken), do not use 'got' alone (without preceding 'have'/'has').
- Remember: The negation of 'have' is 'do not have' and the negation of 'have got' is 'have not got'.
- Never use: 'Silas hasn't a sister.' → Instead, use: 'Silas does not have a sister.'

b) Write the negation of the following statements in formal English (long forms).

1. I have got time to read the paper today.	
2. She has blue eyes.	

2 REGISTER AND STYLE Fill in the corresponding formal expression.
- Do not use slang, sub-standard or colloquial/informal words and expressions in your texts.
- Do not use incorrect grammar – even though you might have heard it in songs or movies.

informal	formal	informal	formal
1. kid		4. This ain't right.	
2. guy, dude		5. I got a headache.	
3. cop		6. He didn't see nothing.	

TIP

Use of tenses for describing literature and visuals
- When writing about a novel or other literature, use the simple present tense.
- When you describe what is going on and what people/characters are doing in a cartoon or photo, use the simple present progressive. Example: In the photo you can see a man who **is playing** the guitar.

3 BRITISH VS. AMERICAN ENGLISH Don't mix AE and BE; choose one variety. Fill in the gaps.

British English	American English	British English	American English
1. centre, theatre		4.	traveling, traveled
2.	color, neighbor	5. flat, lift	
3. defence, offence		6.	truck, freeway

Preparing for evaluation tasks – writing an essay

TIP

General tips

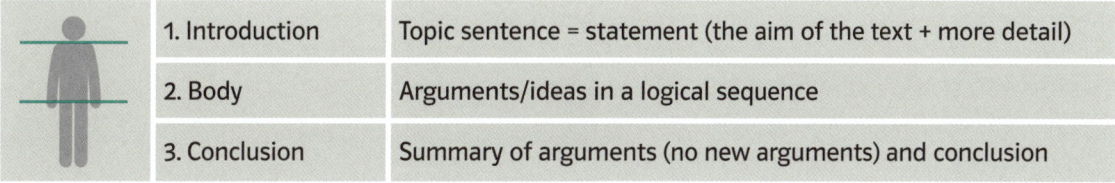

	1. Introduction	Topic sentence = statement (the aim of the text + more detail)
	2. Body	Arguments/ideas in a logical sequence
	3. Conclusion	Summary of arguments (no new arguments) and conclusion

1. Use the **three-part structure** shown above.
2. You can often write the **introductory topic sentence** by rephrasing the task. Ask a rhetorical question that you can answer in the body and return to in the conclusion.
4. Write compact '**SSC' paragraphs:**
   state (the topic sentence) – **support (with evidence/explanation)** – **conclusion/comment**
5. Use **adverbs of comment/degree** (e.g. "luckily"/"mainly") to stress some points → **20.1**
6. When **quoting**, name the source(s) and be careful with the punctuation! → **S12.4**
7. 'Signpost' your ideas by linking sentences and paragraphs with **connectives**.
8. Make your own lists of '**sentence starters**' (useful phrases) to use appropriately. → **S23.4**
9. In your conclusion, **return to the key words** in the question. Close with a prediction for the future, questions still open or a balanced decision.

4 ESSAY TYPES Match these text types with their definitions: argumentative essay • comment • review

a) giving your opinion on a topic → S14.2 _____

b) giving a critical appraisal of a book, film, play etc. → S16 _____

c) presenting a controversial topic by discussing different points of view → S14.1 _____

5 WORKING WITH STRUCTURAL ELEMENTS
a) Note which essay type is required for this example essay task. _____
b) Use coloured markers to highlight the parts of this example essay mentioned in the nine tips.

Example task: Assess which of the problems caused by rainforest deforestation are the most urgent.

Rainforests are disappearing rapidly. Naturally, problems arise when these unique tropical forests are cut down. But which of them are the most urgent?

5 Sadly, one result of deforestation is that more than half of the world's animals are endangered. The tree kangaroo and the jaguar are almost extinct. Animals play an important role in the forests; for example, the spider monkey for seed 10 dispersal. So if these animals die, not only the food chain, but also plant survival will be affected.

Furthermore, food from plants like avocados, guavas, bananas or pineapples can no longer be 15 harvested in these forests if they are cut down.

Medicines and other products are made using plants from the forests as well. We lose valuable resources if we clear forest areas.

The most worrying effect of all, however, is that when logging companies cut down these 20 trees, they are also cutting the great ability of these trees to absorb carbon dioxide. According to the WWF, 15% of all greenhouse gas emissions are a result of deforestation. We simply can't afford to lose more trees. 25

Although it may seem most urgent to save the climate, the whole interconnected ecosystem is vital for a healthy planet. Consequently, we need to save animals, plants and the air that we breathe. 30

c) On p. 114, make your own lists of connectives in these functional categories:

addition • contrast • similarity • exemplification • chronology • causality • attitude • summary

6 YOUR TURN Find essay questions on the topic you are revising and practise writing answers.

After writing – checking for mistakes

Test yourself: Take an essay you have written and check it for common exam mistakes with these tips, refreshing your skills with the tasks. Next to each tip, add examples of your own and note (in pencil) how well you already use these language elements; e.g. ☺, ☺ or ☹. Each time you write a new essay, check whether you have made improvements and adjust your self-assessment.

7 SPELLING RULES Add examples of your own and assess yourself.

TIP	Examples (Use a dictionary for help!)	Assess yourself
Spelling rules • All English words ending in 'ful' are always spelled with one 'l'.	useful, hopeful,	
• We advise: Be wise – when in doubt, use (British English) '-ise'. **Exceptions:** analyse, …	realise, standardise, BUT catalyse,	
• Capitalise names, countries, languages, titles, etc. … and the first person pronoun 'I'.	Do you speak English?;	
• Remember: "he, she, it – 's' muss mit!"	he uses …, she hopes …,	

8 WHERE TO PUT COMMAS Read the tips and examples, practise more and assess yourself.

TIP	Examples	Assess yourself
Commas • A comma must be used after an if-clause … … and before 'which' and 'who' in a non-defining relative clause.	If I had done more revision, I … If I had been …, … My favourite play is *Macbeth*, which …, … Boris Johnson, who …, …	
• In English, no comma is used before 'because' and before 'that' and 'who' in a defining relative clause.	The coursebook is good because it has interesting texts about … I think that …/She is the person who …	

9 POSSESSIVE APOSTROPHES Look carefully at these examples indicating possession and write down the rule in your own words.

That one is Larry's garage • It's Silas's car • Mrs Jones's car is blue • The witness's car is green • The girls' room is over there • The children's books are here • That's the Smiths' house.

Rule:

_____

_____

_____

_____

Assess yourself

10 LOOK OUT FOR MISTRANSLATIONS Write a correct formulation.

Mistranslations (!)	Correct formulation	Assess yourself
The words are ~~standing~~ on the wall. The cartoon was drawn by a ~~drawer~~. from ~~dishwasher to millionaire~~		

11 FALSE FRIENDS Fill in the gaps in the table. Then note down more false friends.

German word	correct English	False friend (!)	German meaning	Assess yourself
aktuell	*current/topical*	actual	eigentlich	
Chef		chef	Chefkoch	
Handy		handy	useful	
sensibel		sensible	vernünftig	
sympathisch		sympathetic	mitfühlend	

12 FREQUENT MIX-UPS

a) These verbs often get mixed up by German native speakers. Fill in the correct words.

1. get (= erhalten) ǂ become (werden)	2. let (zulassen) ǂ make (veranlassen)	3. make ǂ do

1. At the Montagues' party, Romeo and Juliet _____ friends.

   We never _____ homework on Fridays.

2. The old man _____ the boy work hard, but he _____ him drive his car.

3. I try not to _____ mistakes and I usually _____ my homework.

Assess yourself

1. _____

2. _____

3. _____

b) In English there are some words (homophones) that may almost sound the same, but are spelled differently. Write a sentence for each.

there ǂ their ǂ they're • where ǂ were ǂ we're ǂ (to) wear •
your ǂ you're • his ǂ he's • hers ǂ here's • its ǂ it's • two ǂ to ǂ too •
no ǂ (to) know ǂ now • by ǂ (to) buy ǂ bye • than ǂ then • of ǂ off •
here ǂ (to) hear • (to) lose ǂ loose (adjective) • hole ǂ whole •
week ǂ weak • peace ǂ piece • which ǂ witch •
(to) save ǂ safe (adjective) • (to) prove ǂ proof • (to) believe ǂ belief •
(to) live ǂ live (adjective) ǂ life (n.) • (to) accept ǂ (to) expect ǂ except (for)

TIP

Check how you use these plural noun forms!
- For common **uncountable** nouns (e.g. advice, evidence, information and news) use the singular form. Examples: Good advice is invaluable. • That news is awful!
- Some nouns can be **singular or plural**; e.g. the government, the media. Choose one form and use it throughout your text. For "the US", use the singular.
- Don't forget the **irregular** plural forms; e.g. man – men • woman – women • child – children • person – people • life – lives • crisis – crises

Assess yourself

13 IRREGULAR VERBS Write down the three correct verb forms. Assess yourself and practise more.

broadcast   catch   fight   hit   pay   say   teach   think

TIP

Style tips: Make sure that . . .
- your sentences are logical, complete (including a full verb) and not too long.
- you use some passive constructions.
- you don't overuse words like these: part | thing | they (state who you're referring to!) | do | get | go | have | like | put | say | take | think | bad | big | funny | good | important | interesting | nice
- Make lists of synonyms and practise using them in different contexts.

Speaking – Tips for oral exams

14 CHECK YOUR DISCUSSION SKILLS (DIALOGUE)

a) Highlight key words in these tips and add these useful phrases in the gaps to illustrate the tip.

> I have three points to make. Firstly, … • May I interrupt you for a second? • What exactly do you mean by … ? • This is an important point, isn't it? • I think you might be mistaken there. • I would like to come back to what you said about … • That sounds very convincing.

1. Take turns speaking – one person speaks at a time.

2. Listen carefully and attentively to other speakers.

3. Maintain eye contact with the speaker.

4. Use supportive gestures and body language, like nodding to show approval, and encouraging facial expressions, like smiling. You can use supportive phrases too: _____

   _____

5. Structure what you have to say using enumeration: _____

6. Use respectful phrases to disagree with another speaker: _____

7. Interrupt politely by saying something like this: _____

8. Ask questions when you do not understand: _____

9. Interact with your partner by picking up on a point they have made: _____

   _____

10. Keep the ball rolling. Question tags can help you to do this: _____

b) Make your own lists of sentence starters. Practise them in an imagined discussion. → **S23.4**

15 SPEAKING ALONE (MONOLOGUE) All the tips above apply to speaking with others, but which points are also important when speaking alone? Make notes.

_____

16 PRESENTATION PROMPTS You may be asked to describe a picture or a photo (→ **S27.1**) or other visuals like cartoons (→ **27.2**) or diagrams, statistics, maps (→ **S26.1**) and infographics (→ **26.2**).
Practise the four I–D–A–E steps with this photo.

TIP

The four steps I-D-A-E
1. **Introduction:** State the theme in one sentence.
2. **Description:** What can you see and where? → **S27**
   - Comment on speech bubbles, captions, signs and people's facial expressions.
   - Use the simple present for objects and the setting and the present progressive for people's actions.
3. **Analysis:** Speculate on and analyse the message, target group or the elements supporting the message.
4. **Evaluation:** Is this visual effective? Give your personal opinion or thoughts.

17 PRACTICE Choose visual prompts relevant to your revision topics. Work with useful phrases to describe, analyse and evaluate them. Try recording yourself or practise with a friend. What can you improve upon?

Facts

Identity in a diverse world

1 THE SELF AND IDENTITY Give short answers.

1. State whether the concepts of the self and identity are related or not.

   _____

2. To what extent are the self and identity social products?

   _____

   _____

3. How does feedback from others affect one's actions?

   _____

   _____

2 WORLDWIDE MIGRATION Fill in the gaps with these words:

| intracontinental | mother | war | global | permanently | intercontinental | constant |

Migration refers to people moving _____ or temporarily, usually from their

_____ country to another one. Surprisingly for some, migration has been

relatively _____ over time, except in times of _____

or after natural disasters. _____ migration is most common, although

_____ migration to Europe has increased since WWII. According to Guy Abel's

chord diagram of _____ migration, 271.6 million people now live outside their

country of birth.

3 WHAT DRIVES MIGRATION Match the sentence parts.

1 Push and pull models are a simplistic way to
2 Push factors like poverty or war
3 Such models fail to
4 Recent research describes migration as
5 The factual wage disparity may 'push and pull',
6 In this context, education and access to it

- [ ] A a function of capabilities and aspirations.
- [ ] B play an important role.
- [ ] C but the migrant must grasp the opportunity.
- [ ] D interact with pull factors like security.
- [ ] E explain migration movements.
- [ ] F take migrants' active role into account.

4 MIGRATION IN GERMANY AND EUROPE Complete the grid with notes for a possible exam question on developments related to migration in Germany and Europe.

Germany	Europe

Choices in work and society

1 GAP YEAR

a) Make a mind map with the title 'Gap year' and these main branches:

> experimental learning   effects   keys to success

b) Add these notes as sub-branches:

> saved money for education • backpacking • volunteering • internships abroad • improved
> employability • better understanding of what course to study • careful planning • structure •
> deepened awareness

c) Add these details to the appropriate sub-branches:

> practical   personal   professional   soft skills   résumé/CV

2 UNIVERSITY EDUCATION IN THE US AND EUROPE Make notes about the following three points.
Then write statements for each point to form a continuous text.
1. specialised national degrees vs. BA/MA programmes, 2. international standards and effects
on job-hunting, and 3. tuition fees in Germany, the US and the UK.

3 THREE-SECTOR THEORY Fill in the gaps with these words:

> manufacturing • agriculture • unemployment • manual labour • subdivisions • advanced •
> low-cost • white-collar • relocation • services

All economic activity can be classified into three _____ : 1. primary sector (mining or

_____), 2. secondary sector (_____), and 3. tertiary sector

(_____). In the more _____ economies tertiary employment is

higher. Blue-collar employment is characterised by _____ , whereas a

_____ worker is typically employed in an office, better educated and better paid.

_____ among blue-collar workers is a greater threat as globalisation has seen the

_____ of production lines to _____ countries.

4 AUTOMATION True or false? Make notes to correct any false statements below.

	True	False
1. Automation is the technology that reduces the number of people and the time to manufacture a product and, therefore, the cost.		
2. Automation is more accurate and reliable.		
3. It makes work less monotonous for the workforce.		
4. Over time, it will increase the number of jobs.		
5. Digitalisation is for services what automation is for manufacturing.		

Corrections: _____

_____

5 GENDER Make notes to describe the following terms..

1. Gender inequality _____

2. Traditional family roles _____

3. Gender gap_____

The media

1 FROM ANALOGUE TO DIGITAL MEDIA Multiple choice: Tick the false option.

1. Before the 21st century, …

☐ a) 'phone' meant landline.

☐ b) radio programmes weren't streamed.

☐ c) letters were mailed with stamps.

☐ d) books were paperless.

2. Before the advent of digital media, people …

☐ a) had more haptic and personal interactions.

☐ b) listened to music through loudspeakers.

☐ c) often watched reality TV shows together.

☐ d) had a different idea of 'socialising'.

3. With analogue media you had …

☐ a) to make a tape of a song to share it.

☐ b) a lot less privacy than today.

☐ c) to go to a library for information.

☐ d) fewer TV programmes than we do now.

4. In a digital world people …

☐ a) can publish their opinions on social media.

☐ b) can publish fake news.

☐ c) must have their photos reviewed by an editor.

☐ d) don't have to be professionally trained reporters.

2 SOCIAL MEDIA AND POLITICS Short answers: Make notes.

1. How has social media changed the way elections are run for politicians and the public?

_____

_____

2. How does the sharing of information between members of the public on social networks contribute to polarisation in society?

_____

_____

3 PRIVATE AND PUBLIC FUNDING Fill in the gaps with these items:

> platforms • viral marketing • pop-up banners • internet-based • influencers • public • licence fee • videos • subscribers • digital • traditional

Spending on _____ advertisements overtook _____ media ad expenses for the first time in 2019. Customised ads via messages or _____ are the biggest source of revenue for many large _____ companies. Furthermore, social media _____ insert ads into _____, story content or users' newsfeeds. Such _____ methods are extremely popular with advertisers, as the message spreads quickly. Businesses also recruit _____ and celebrities to endorse products on their social media sites. _____ broadcasting services finance their TV, radio and internet programmes with a _____ (and some advertising), which helps them to remain largely free of commercial and political interests. Commercial broadcasting is financed by _____ or, if it is "free", by advertising.

Tradition and change in the UK

1 THE HISTORY OF THE UK
Draw and annotate a timeline to illustrate the history of the UK.

2 THE BRITISH EMPIRE
You can use notes to make other word clouds (using an app) about periods in history relevant to your Abi revision. In this example, write individual sentences or link them in a paragraph about the history of the British Empire.

3 THE NORTH-SOUTH DIVIDE Make notes in the bullet list below about the North-South divide in England and use them to write a text in answer to this task:
Comment on the statement, "The 'North-South divide' in England is a reflection of a disunited Kingdom."

- _____   - _____
- _____   - _____
- _____   - _____

4 IMMIGRATION Say something about Immigration and Britishness using these ideas:

> ethnically and culturally diverse • labour shortages in the 50s and 60s • East Midlands and the North • debate on limits and benefits of migration • British identity • British citizenship

5 THE POLITICAL SYSTEM IN THE UNITED KINGDOM Make notes on the political system in the UK in the mind map. Use the mind map to record a short talk on the UK political system.

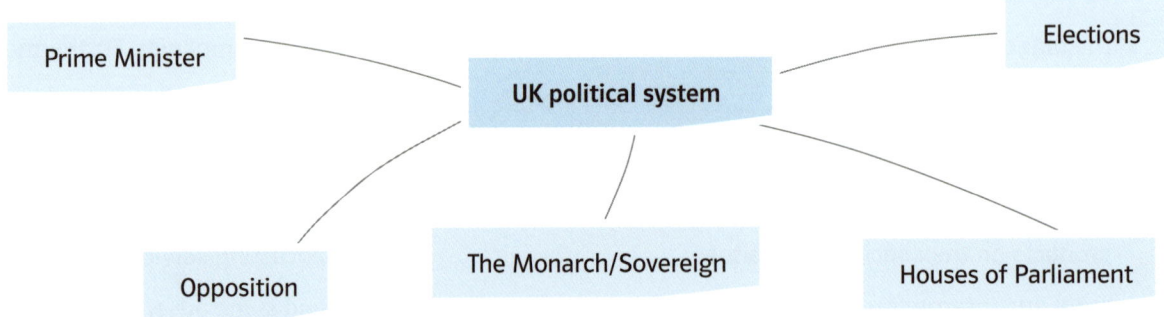

6 UK AND THE EU Describe the relationship between the UK and the EU now.

The US – a diverse nation

1 **THE MAKING OF A NATION** On p. 115, make a timeline of historic events in US history using these dates. Add the events to the correct years. Do some research if necessary.

> c. 13,000 BC • 1492 • after 1600 • by the 1770s • 1773 • 1775–1783 • 4th July 1776 • 1787 •
> 1848 and 1845-1852 • 1861–1865 • 1865 • 1896 • 1924 • 1950s–60s • 1963 • 2008 • 2013 • 2021

> Civil Rights Movement • American Constitution is written • Boston Tea Party •
> Indigenous cultures already living on the American continent • European colonists begin to arrive
> in America • first Black vice-president (Kamala Harris) • the Civil War • 13 British colonies on the
> north-eastern coast • introduction of Jim Crow laws in southern states • March on Washington and
> "I Have a Dream" speech (Martin Luther King) • Christopher Columbus discovers America • beginning of
> Black Lives Matter movement • large-scale immigration from Germany and Ireland • abolition of
> slavery • Revolutionary War (War of Independence) • first Black president (Barack Obama) •
> Native Americans recognised as US citizens with the right to vote • Declaration of Independence signed

2 **THE AMERICAN DREAM**

a) Create a mind map about the American Dream using key words and terms from the chapter as well as your own ideas.

b) Do you believe the American Dream is alive today? You may use key words.

_____

_____

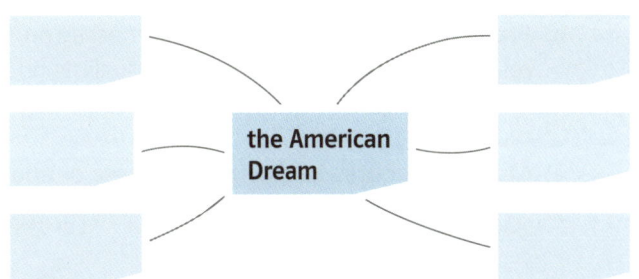

the American Dream

3 **THE US POLITICAL SYSTEM** Fill in the gaps using these words:

> "checks and balances" • Democratic Party • elections • legislative branch • executive branch •
> US capital • judicial branch • Republican Party • US Constitution • US presidents

The United States is a federal constitutional republic. The _____ , ratified in 1790,

gives the individual states enough authority to prevent the federal government from becoming too

powerful. Furthermore, the Constitution specifies the three branches of the federal government: the

_____ (the Administration), the _____ (the Supreme Court),

and the _____ (Congress, which in turn consists of the House of Representatives

and the US Senate). Moreover, each branch can control the others' decisions. This system of

_____ prevents the abuse of power by any branch. The _____ ,

Washington D.C., is home to all three government headquarters.

Presidential _____ are held every four years. First, each party's candidate is chosen

in a long process starting with primaries or caucuses. Then, on Election Day, US citizens elect the members

of the Electoral College. _____ , who are at the same time head of state and head of

government, serve the nation for no more than two consecutive terms.

The two main parties in the US Congress are the 'blue' _____ (more liberal) and the

'red' _____ (more conservative). There are traditionally 'red', 'blue' or 'swing' states;

many large cities tend to be 'blue', whereas most rural areas are 'red'.

India

1 COLONISATION AND INDEPENDENCE

a) Make brief notes to complete the table of events in India.

Date	Event/Notes
Before 1858	
1858 (–1947)	
1876	
1914 and inter-war years	
18th July 1947	
1972	

b) Prepare a short talk or write a short essay on: Partition and its aftermath. In doing so, briefly outline the relationship between Hindus and Muslims on the Indian subcontinent today.

2 INDIA TODAY

a) Make short notes on themes like these or another theme of your choice:

Geography   Climate   Population   Language   Economy   Politics

_____

_____

_____

b) Inform yourself in greater detail about the political and economic situation in India today.

3 INDIA'S MAIN RELIGIONS

a) Match the percentages of India's people with their religions.

1 Sikh
2 Muslim
3 Buddhist
4 Hindu
5 Christian
6 Jain

☐ A 1.7%
☐ B 0.4%
☐ C 80%
☐ D 0.7%
☐ E 14%
☐ F 2.3%

b) Use these terms to fill in the gaps:

Brahma   Holi   the destroyer   triumvirate   karma   900 million   Samsara   the preserver

Hinduism is the oldest living religion with more than _____ believers worldwide.

_____ (reincarnation) is governed by one's _____ (actions

and their effects). God, the supreme being, has many different aspects and incarnations, but the three

most important ones are: Shiva (_____), _____ (the creator)

and Vishnu (_____). These three gods are referred to as the Hindu

_____. There are many religious festivals, such as _____.

Global challenges

1 GLOBALISATION Give a short definition of globalisation in your own words.

_____

_____

_____

2 THE THREE PHASES OF GLOBALISATION Match the corresponding information.

1 Phase 1 15th–19th century	**A** goods from all over the world available anywhere; multinational corporations; abolition of tariffs; creation of free trade zones; neo-liberal capitalist world-order; free trade of goods, services and people across Europe and most parts of the world
2 Phase 2 20th century	**B** digitalisation of communication and work processes; participation in global economic process
3 Phase 3 21st century	**C** colonisation of India and Africa by the major European powers; discovery of America

3 CHANCES AND CHALLENGES OF GLOBALISATION

a) Group these items by determining which perspective they represent: economic, ecological or cultural perspective?

A economic perspective   **B** ecological perspective   **C** cultural perspective

- [C] **1** cheap access to global communication (internet)
- [ ] **2** secure jobs, livelihoods, and economic stability
- [ ] **3** higher (industrial) production leads to more industrial waste
- [ ] **4** increasing need for water leads to freshwater shortage
- [ ] **5** companies have access to cheaper materials and labour
- [ ] **6** connectedness facilitates trade cooperation and access to information
- [ ] **7** poor or remote places have less access to online opportunities
- [ ] **8** companies practise outsourcing and offshoring
- [ ] **9** increase in food production harms the environment
- [ ] **10** global players dominate the (global) market
- [ ] **11** global communication enables the emergence of a global civil society
- [ ] **12** transporting raw materials globally increases air pollution
- [ ] **13** tax evasion, stagnating wages in developed countries
- [ ] **14** global communication makes sensitive personal data available
- [ ] **15** lower costs, higher profits for companies

b) Think of further aspects that match any of the three perspectives. It may help to take a close look at the corresponding chapter in your student book or to do some research online.

c) Use green to highlight the positive effects and red for the negative ones. Try to leave no items unmarked.

Science and visions of the future

1 ARTIFICIAL INTELLIGENCE (AI)

a) Give a brief definition of Artificial Intelligence and its two different systems.

_____

_____

b) Give examples of the domains in which AI can be used. If you need information going beyond the text, do some online research.

_____

_____

2 AI – A BLESSING OR A CURSE?

a) Reflect on the chances and challenges of AI and complete the chart below.

Chances of Artificial Intelligence	Challenges of Artificial Intelligence
1. _____ _____	1. _____ _____
2. _____ _____	2. _____ _____
3. _____ _____	3. _____ _____

b) Discuss the chances and the challenges of AI in an argumentative essay. → S14.1

3 AUGMENTED REALITY (AR) AND VIRTUAL REALITY (VR)

a) Have you ever used augmented or virtual reality in your own life? In which domain was it? Share your personal experiences with a partner or describe it in an email to a friend.

b) Analyse the chart about users of augmented and virtual reality in the Spot on facts in your _Green Line Oberstufe_ book.

4 UTOPIA OR DYSTOPIA

a) Where will technology take us? Explain the terms "utopia" and "dystopia" and their aims.

Utopia	Dystopia
_____	_____
_____	_____
_____	_____
_____	_____

b) Be creative and think of further topics for a utopian or dystopian novel.

_____

_____

_____

Shakespeare

1 SHAKESPEARE'S LIFE AND TIMES On this mind map of Shakespeare's life and times, add around these prompts all the useful information you can find on the Spot on facts pages in your coursebook.

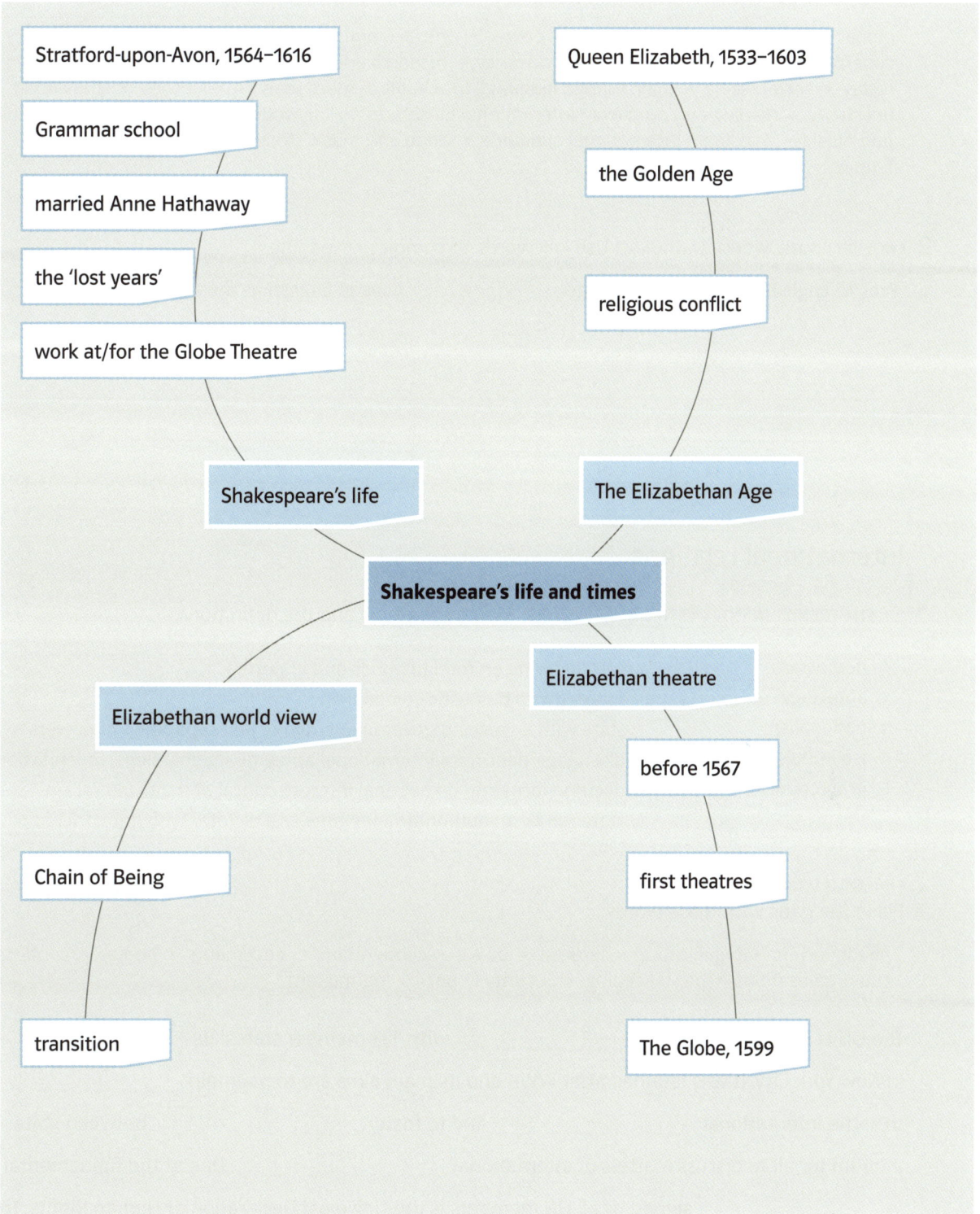

2 WRITING AND TALKING ABOUT SHAKESPEARE

a) Use your mind map to write a short text or give a talk about the different aspects of Shakespeare's life and times. If you speak, try recording what you say, and then listen to it again (– and again) to revise the content. Do not forget to use your background knowledge to go into greater detail.

b) Practise whatever is important for your Abi revision. For example, maybe you will want to make your own mind map about a play, a character or themes in Shakespeare's plays **or** make a timeline using these dates and add the events for the correct years. Do more research if necessary.

The Englishes

1 REASONS WHY ENGLISH IS THE WORLD LANGUAGE Make a mind map with the categories "history", "business", "politics", "education", "entertainment" and "science and technology" and fill the blanks in the mind map using the terms below.

global trade • USA as global economic power • official language in 55 states • USA a global superpower • dollar as global reserve currency • research and technology • the internet • Silicon Valley • social media • main foreign language in schools in more than 100 countries • studying at university • reading and producing international literature • Hollywood films • American and British pop music • maximum international audience • video and music streaming services • British Empire • British colonies

2 ENGLISH AS THE WORLD LANGUAGE Use key words to complete the table.

Pros of English as the world language	Cons of English as the world language

International relations

1 RECENT TRENDS IN INTERNATIONAL RELATIONS Match the terms and the definitions.

1 democracy
2 autocracy
3 nationalism
4 isolationism
5 protectionism

- [ ] A setting tariffs on foreign goods and imports to safeguard domestic companies
- [ ] B state with an elected government, rule of law, separation of powers
- [ ] C disengagement from international agreements, coalitions, organisations
- [ ] D doctrine focussing on national interest, critical of multiculturalism
- [ ] E state run by an authoritarian regime or a dictator with unrestricted power

2 THE UNITED NATIONS
a) Fill in the gaps with these words:

headquarters • organisation • interest • peace • cooperation • documents • bodies • conflicts • sub-organisations • peacekeeping • Security Council • permanent

The UN is an international _____ with 193 member states. Its _____ are in New York City. It was founded after WWII and its main aims are to maintain _____,
to settle international _____ and to foster _____ between states. It is also a forum for all to discuss matters of international _____ . One of the fundamental _____ signed by all UN members is the Universal Declaration of Human Rights. The main _____ of the UN are the General Assembly and the _____ , which are made up of five _____ (USA, Russia, China, UK and France) and ten non-permanent members. It includes various _____ like UNICEF (United Nations Children's Fund) and WHO (World Health Organisation). The UN also conducts _____ operations around the world.

b) Make notes (key words) to explain why nowadays the UN is more important than ever before.

Canada and New Zealand

1 COMMON GROUND

a) Look at these key words and decide whether they belong to Canada or New Zealand or both.
Write them in the appropriate column in the table below.

> Aotearoa • member of the UN • Canada Day • Kiwis • Waitangi Day • second-largest country in the
> world • Ottawa • Auckland • Quebec • Nunavut • North Island • South Island • English is the
> main/most widely used language • Māori/Te Reo Māori • bilingual country • First Nations • Métis •
> Inuit/Inuktitut • 38 million inhabitants • 5 million inhabitants • home to many different ethnic and
> cultural groups • member of the Commonwealth • haka • the Maple Leaf • All Blacks and Black Ferns •
> Yukon multicultural society • Northwest Territories • six time zones • earthquakes and volcanoes •
> beaver • moose • tā moko • mountie • high standard of living

Canada	both	New Zealand
Canada Day,...	*member of the UN, ...*	*Aotearoa, ...*

b) Choose one option and complete the sentence. You may use key words.

I would like to …

☐ a) travel to Canada …

☐ b) work in Canada (for a while) …

☐ c) immigrate to Canada …

☐ d) travel to New Zealand …

☐ e) work in New Zealand (for a while) …

☐ f) immigrate to New Zealand …

because

Ecological challenges

1 SUSTAINABLE DEVELOPMENT GOALS

a) List as many of the 17 United Nations sustainable development goals as possible.

_____

_____

_____

_____

_____

_____

_____

_____

_____

_____

_____

b) Circle or highlight the three goals that you consider to be most important. Explain your choice.

1. _____

_____

2. _____

_____

3. _____

_____

2 ENVIRONMENT AND HUMAN HEALTH Fill in the gaps using these words:

> endangered • extinction • temperatures • impact • global warming • privileged • slash-and-burn •
> sustainability • responsibility

The present era, called the Anthropocene, witnesses the highest _____ rate of living

species ever. This is caused by the enormous expansion of urban areas worldwide and

_____ practices used to clear land for farming and animal husbandry (e.g. cattle farms).

Consequently, more than 60 % of _____ animal species are currently at risk. More than one

million animal and plant species (1/8 of all species on the planet) are in danger of extinction in the near

future.

Global average _____ are rising because of air pollution, greenhouse gases and the

increasing concentration of CO_2 in the atmosphere. This phenomenon, known as _____,

leads to extreme weather events, which have a detrimental _____. Heatwaves, droughts,

hurricanes, heavy downpours and floods pose an imminent threat to humanity.

More and more people around the world are taking _____ by making informed decisions

in order to promote _____ and reduce the impacts of climate change and pollution.

Nevertheless, there is no denying the fact that the poor and less _____ seem to suffer the

most from climate change and pollution.

Skills

Reading

1 SQ3R Fill in the gaps with these words:

| recite | understand | practise | remember | technique | question | survey | exam |

There are two things we need to do when reading; one is to _____ and the other is

to _____ what we have read. SQ3R is a reading _____ with

the following steps: _____ , _____ , read, _____ ,

review. You should _____ using this technique with any text you read as often as

you can. In an _____ you will need to do things quickly.

2 THE 5 STEPS Match the points (1.–3.) with the different steps.

STEP 1 Survey	☐	1 Having read the paragraph, ask yourself the question you formulated. 2 Make notes/highlight key words to help answer your question. 3 Use your own words, if possible, when making notes.
STEP 2 Question	☐	1 Take a very short break before the next step – a drink, something to eat. 2 Go over the whole text again, one paragraph after the other. 3 First state the theme and then summarise the main content of each part.
STEP 3 Read	☐	1 Get a good overview. 2 Look for headings, sub-headings, pictures, graphs, etc. 3 Skim your reading material.
STEP 4 Recite	☐	1 Stay relaxed and concentrated. 2 With your question in mind, read one paragraph at a time carefully. 3 Look for information to answer your question.
STEP 5 Review	☐	1 What seems to be the main theme? 2 Scan each paragraph. Try to sum up the content in one sentence. 3 Turn the sentence into a question.

3 READING FASTER True or false? Tick the appropriate box. Make notes below to explain why a statement is wrong.

	True	False
1. All sections of a text are equally important.		
2. Good articles are well-structured like this: The first sentence states the idea, and the final sentence sums up the paragraph. The others support and develop the idea.		
3. You can save time by focusing on the middle part of the paragraph.		

_____

4 COMMAND WORDS (Operatoren) Match the command words with what they ask you to do.

1 Describe	☐ A	Give the main features/structure/general principles of something.
2 Outline	☐ B	Give a concise account of the main points/ideas of a text/topic/issue.
3 Summarise	☐ C	Give a detailed account of what someone or something is like.

Mediation

1 A CHECKLIST FOR MEDIATION You can use the checklist for Task 4. First, complete the table with these key words:

register   correctness   addressee   relevant points   comprehension   coherence   target text   purpose

Ask yourself these questions:	Key words	1	2	3
1. Do I understand the text?				
2. Who am I mediating the text for?				
3. Why am I mediating?				
4. What information is important?				
5. What kind of mediation text must I produce?				
6. What type of language must I use? (formal/informal)				
7. Have I used transitions and linking words?				
8. Is my grammar, spelling and punctuation correct?				

2 TIPS FOR MEDIATION Match the two sentence parts.

1	Mediation does not mean	☐	A	rather than a noun.
2	Highlight/Mark relevant information	☐	B	distinguish between different aspects.
3	Use the highlighted information to	☐	C	can be broken down into its parts.
4	Use colour coding to	☐	D	catch the attention of the addressee.
5	Cultural differences may make it necessary to	☐	E	sum up your main points.
6	Paraphrase important words	☐	F	in the original (German) text.
7	Do the paraphrasing	☐	G	when you don't know the exact translation.
8	Sometimes it helps to use a verb	☐	H	translating word for word.
9	A long German word	☐	I	without using a dictionary.
10	Think of an appropriate introduction to	☐	J	make structured notes in English.
11	Don't forget to	☐	K	explain some terms.

3 LINGUISTIC AND IDIOMATIC CHALLENGES Find ways to express these ideas in English:

a) Sie besuchte ein *Gymnasium*. (→ You can explain the cultural difference.)

_____

b) *Leistung* muss belohnt werden. (→ Paraphrase!)

_____

c) Die Zahl der *Studienabbrecher* steigt an. (→ You can use a verb with a relative clause.)

_____

4 MEDIATION PRACTICE Use the checklist in Task 1 above. Tick off the points on the right as you do the mediation tasks (1–3) on your Abi-relevant topics. You can reuse the mediation tasks in your text- and workbook.

Working with images – oral exams

In your oral exam, you will have to give a presentation (monologue). Use the checklists below to help practise structuring your talk with different visuals (e.g. photos, cartoons, charts) on a topic you are revising. Refer to the skills section of your course book for language support (useful phrases). → S22

1 CHECKLIST FOR WORKING WITH VISUALS Tick the points as you work with an image.

Description	1	2	3
1 State the **type** of visual (photo, cartoon, …). Say **what** you can see (in one sentence).			
2 Give the **setting** (time and place) in the simple present.			
3 Describe the visual in **detail**: people, objects, foreground, background. Use the present progressive to describe actions.			

Analysis	1	2	3
1 Examine any people shown. Is there anything special about them?			
2 Look out for symbols (objects, gestures, …). What do they stand for?			
3 Check any text (title, speech/thought/sound bubbles, captions, insets, signs, …). Who is speaking to whom? Why?			
4 Look for the source. What's the context (time/place)?			
5 State the message and the addressee and give your reasons.			

Evaluation	1	2	3
1 Give your personal opinion with reasons.			
2 Make references to your own experience or imagine how you would feel.			
3 Comment on the effectiveness: importance to viewer • comprehensibility of message • humour (e.g. irony, exaggeration) • appeal (e.g. boring, eye-catching).			

2 CHECKLIST FOR WORKING WITH CHARTS Tick the points as you work with a chart.

Description	1	2	3
1 **Type** (pie-/bar chart, line graph, infographic)			
2 **Theme** (see title)			
3 Look for **numbers**, **units of measurement**, **categories** and the **time frame**. Describe the x- and y-axis.			
4 State the **source**.			

Analysis	1	2	3
1 Focus on **maximum/minimum points**, **trends**.			
2 You might need to **compare** two charts/graphs.			

Evaluation	1	2	3
1 Consider the **intention** of the author and the **importance** of the data.			
2 Provide a **short conclusion**: It can be seen from the chart that …			

Writing a comment on a non-fictional text

Britain faces a no-deal crash-out : even ultra-Brexiters said this would be a disaster

Perhaps we're so hardened, or punch-drunk, after a year of being battered by the pandemic that we don't quite register how shocking this is. We stand on the brink of a no-deal crash-out from the European Union: the very outcome that all but the most extreme Brexiters once agreed would be a catastrophe for this country, an outcome our leaders insisted would never happen.

Jonathan Freedland, *The Guardian*, 2020

1 USE OF LANGUAGE AND RHETORICAL DEVICES Having read the title and the opening paragraph of the newspaper article, it is immediately clear what Jonathan Freedland thinks of a no-deal Brexit. But how does his use of language and rhetorical devices help him to achieve this? Match the language and rhetorical devices with the examples using the colour code in the text. → S10

| nouns | adjectives | anaphora | figurative language | emphasis |

2 TONE

a) Which of these adjectives could be used to describe the tone of the article/the author's attitude to the topic he is writing about? In your opinion, which word is the best one to use?

| incensed | enthusiastic | compassionate | humorous | ironic | serious | critical | positive | scathing |

b) Search the internet for other words to describe an author's tone.

3 WRITING A COMMENT Read the tips in the table and highlight what you think are the key points.

Preparation	Form your opinion. Collect arguments – and also possible counterarguments – and how you can refute them. Structure your essay with an outline plan (weakest arguments first, strongest last). Make a quick exam plan with enough time at the end for a final check.
Writing	Use a structure of three parts and present your arguments in paragraphs. → S12.1 **Introduction:** Present the issue and catch the reader's attention. **Body:** If you disagree, you can start by agreeing in part. Then present counterarguments and finish with your strongest arguments. If you agree, add more examples to support the author's points – weakest to strongest! **Conclusion:** Summarise your opinion and give an outlook on further developments or possible solutions; but do not add new ideas.
Edit/Check	Edit and check your text for cohesion, language, rhetorical devices, etc. → S12.2

4 EXPRESSING AN OPINION OR COUNTERING ARGUMENTS

a) Complete the table below with these sentence starters:

| I strongly question … | As far as I can see, … | There is no doubt that … |

| The author has a point, but … | It might be argued that … | This certainly sounds good. However, … |

Expressing opinions/Convincing people	Countering arguments
_____	_____
_____	_____
_____	_____

b) Make your own language bank and add other sentence starters and useful phrases which you might use in an answer to a comment question. Think about useful phrases to sum up too. → S14

Analysing non-fictional texts and writing an argumentative essay

Checklist for analysing a non-fictional text

☐ 1. What is the text type (e.g. (auto)biography, news article, editorial, …)?

☐ 2. What can you say about the author?

☐ 3. Who is the addressee?

☐ 4. What is its purpose/function? (expository, descriptive, argumentative/persuasive, instructive)

☐ 5. What is the writer's perspective and their relationship with the audience?

☐ 6. Identify the tone and style and their effect.

☐ 7. What linguistic devices are used? What is their effect?

☐ 8. What is the main effect on the reader?

1 PRACTICE Choose one or more text extracts related to the topic you are revising. Refer to the checklist above and write an analysis of your chosen text/s. The useful phrases in the Abi skills workshop in the US topic will help you too.

2 WRITING AN ARGUMENTATIVE ESSAY Complete the gap text with these words:
3-part • SWOT • opposing • dialectical • ideas/information • edit • chronological • assess • similarities/differences • neutral • logical • enumerative

Command words like discuss, _____ or evaluate require you to write an

argumentative essay in which you present a controversial topic from _____ points

of view in a clear and _____ way. Collect _____ with at least

three arguments for/against the issue in question. A _____ analysis can help you

(Strengths • Weaknesses • Opportunities • Threats). There are different approaches you can take when

planning your essay: a) a _____ approach with negative, and then positive

arguments or, alternatively, an argument followed by a counterargument; b) _____

order; c) a comparative approach (_____); d) an _____

approach (list). Ask yourself what your aim is. Is it to persuade the reader to agree with you or do you want

to remain _____ ? Write your essay with a _____ structure: an

introduction, the main part, the body, with paragraphs (→ S12.1) and a conclusion. (→ S14.1) As a final step,

_____ your text. (→ S12.2)

3 EXPRESSING IDEAS Put these useful phrases in the categories listed in the table below. Make your own table and add other sentence starters/useful phrases. → S14.1

> The long-term consequences are … • On balance, it is clear that … • And here's what really is at stake: … • There are (two) issues to consider here, namely … • In other words, … • Conversely, it could be argued that … • This also raises questions about … • … will lead to …

Presenting aspects and examples	_____
Using connectives → S12.1	_____
Talking about developments/results	_____
Summing up/Conclusion	_____

Analysing fictional texts

1 A FICTIONAL TEXT Fill in the gaps with these words:

> interact • scene • characters • traits • action • setting • relationships • authors • plot • events • narrator

_____ write fictional novels, but they choose a _____ to tell

the story of their imaginary _____ and the _____ that occur.

The _____ refers to where (the _____) and when the

_____ takes place. As the _____ develops, the characters

behave in certain ways and _____ with each other. The reader can examine

individual character _____ and the _____ between characters.

2 NARRATIVE PERSPECTIVE

a) Match the narrator with the point of view (= the perspective from which the reader experiences the story).

| 1 first-person | A unlimited point of view |

| | B speaks as "I" (or "we") |

| 2 third-person observer – outside story or central/fringe character | C limited point of view |

| | D an all-knowing observer outside the story |

| 3 third-person omniscient | E speaks about others as "he", "she", "they" |

b) State the effects of different perspectives on the reader. → S8

> first-person   third-person observer   third-person omniscient

3 CHARACTERS

a) Make notes to define the following types of character:

1. major character _____

2. round character _____

3. flat character _____

b) Authors can describe a character both directly and indirectly. Using colour coding, match **A** (ways a character can be characterised indirectly) with **B** (the text evidence [= quote]) and **C** (the inferred 'character adjective').

A	decisions	actions	thoughts	moods	interactions	personal effects
B	'He was in that dark place again.'	'She held her old mother's hand gently.'	'His room was a real mess.'	'He didn't think about it for a second.'	'In her mind she shrieked, "Oh, no!"'	'He simply hit him.'
C	scared	disorganised	depressed	loving/caring	aggressive	impulsive

c) Do an internet search for 'Character adjectives' - and learn some you think will help you.

Analysing a speech

1 THREE SPEECH ELEMENTS Fill in the gaps: | informative | explanatory | persuasive |

One of the three elements can dominate in a speech, according to its purpose, but speeches often show

elements of all three. _____ elements are intended to show how something works

or why it is effective, whereas with _____ elements the speaker tells the audience

what they know about a topic. Political speeches are usually _____ in character as

the speaker tries to win people over and get them to take action. → S15

2 CHECKLIST Complete the checklist with these missing words:

> tone • arguments • adjectives/verbs • topic • structure • purpose • audience • rhetorical • effect • paralinguistic

1. What main _____ is dealt with in the speech? Who is the

   _____ ?

2. What can you say about the _____ /non-verbal communication (body language,

   gesture, facial expression)?

3. Is there a clear _____ ? What are the main _____ ?

4. What _____ devices are used? What can you say about the overall

   _____ ? Make sure you look at the _____ used in the

   speech. → S10.1

5. What is the _____ of the speech?

6. What _____ does the speech have on you?

3 A PERSUASIVE STRUCTURE Match the details (A–H) with Monroe's five structural key elements (1.–5.):

> A give details/examples • B an anecdote •
> C making positive effects of a solution clear • D a rhetorical question •
> E point out current problem/s • F a welcome •
> G say what must be done • H explain why sth. is ineffective

_F_	1 Attention
_____	2 Need (to)
_____	3 Satisfaction
_____	4 Visualisation
_____	5 Action

4 RHETORICAL DEVICES

a) Match the rhetorical device with the correct example and effect.

Rhetorical device	Example	Effect
Exaggeration/Hyperbole	Firstly, … Secondly, … And finally, …	Connects two different things
Metaphor	I have a dream. I have a dream that…	Increases the power of an idea
Antithesis/Contrast	This will take forever.	Visualises an idea
Enumeration	Patience is bitter, but its fruit is sweet	Emphasises a message
Anaphora	Life is a mountain, not a beach.	Gives structure and clarity

b) Then make a table like this with other rhetorical devices and find examples in Jacinda Ardern's speech (in the Abi skills of the topic Global challenges in your coursebook) to illustrate them. → S10.2

Listening

1 TYPES OF LISTENING TASKS Match what you must do with the task type by putting the right number in the box. Then highlight the closed and semi-open task types in the table. (In a closed task there is one obvious answer. In a semi-open task you are free to choose how to word the answer.)

Task type	What you must do
1 multiple choice	☐ **A** Complete a sentence with a word/phrase/fact.
2 single choice	☐ **B** Choose the correct answer/s from four options. Be careful! In an exam task, it usually says that "Only one answer is correct".
3 matching	☐ **C** Link two parts; e.g. a term and a definition, a statement and the speaker.
4 short answers	
5 table completion	☐ **D** Three pieces of information/ideas have to be connected here.
6 multiple matching	☐ **E** Add notes/facts (key words) to a heading in a grid.
7 sentence completion	☐ **F** Give an answer in note form, not in complete sentences.
8 gap filling	☐ **G** Finish a sentence with the correct information, but not necessarily with the original wording.
	☐ **H** Choose the correct answer from three options.

2 LISTENING STRATEGY

a) Fill in the gaps with these words/phrases:

> break • listenings • guess • title • "firstly" • abbreviations • signposts • stay relaxed • intonation • task mapping • highlight • clever • anticipate • prior knowledge • chronological • elimination

1. _____ . You do not have to understand every word. Focus on what you

   understand. Perhaps the context can help you _____ the meaning.

2. Do careful _____ . Look at the _____ and read

   the tasks. _____ key words in the tasks so you know what to listen for.

3. In an exam situation, there will be two listenings. Note down statistics, dates, etc. and use

   _____ . Spelling in your notes is not important.

4. Remember that the questions usually come in _____ order. If you miss a

   point, you can come back to it on the second listening.

5. What _____ do you have of the topic? Try to _____

   what the general message is and what aspects might be mentioned.

6. Listen to the way the speaker says something. _____ can help you decide

   their attitude or intention. It might be a question, criticism, a suggestion or a joke.

7. Listen out for _____ ; connectives like _____ or "for example".

8. In the _____ between the listenings, check what you still need to focus on.

9. A process of _____ may help you to make a _____

   guess in a multiple choice task.

b) When you have completed the gap text, highlight the key words you think are important.

Analysing a scene from a play

1 A PLAY IS NOT A BOOK. Fill in the gaps with these words:

> actors • atmosphere • contemporary • focus • interpretation • movements • one-act • script • stage directions • tragicomedy

The text of a play is a _____ written to be performed by _____

on a stage or a film set, or perhaps on the radio. The _____ of the original text

involves a number of different aspects including the setting, _____ and ways

of speaking, which influence the action, the _____ and the emotions

expressed. _____ instruct the director/reader about such things, although a

director might choose to change the original setting to address a _____ event

or to change the _____. Terms such as comedy, tragedy and

_____ are used to describe different types of dramatic literature.

There are also _____ plays which, like short stories, focus on one event.

2 FORMAL ELEMENTS Complete the table with the appropriate terms:

> antagonist • climax/turning point • costumes/sound/lighting/props • denouement • exposition • extras • falling action • hero/heroine • indoor/outdoor • major • minor • modern/historical • protagonist • rising action • scenery/backdrop

Structure	Setting	Characters
1. _____	time setting (_____)	_____ ↔ _____
2. _____	• _____	• _____
3. _____	• _____	• _____
4. _____	• _____	• _____
5. _____	• _____	• _____

3 TIPS FOR THE ANALYSIS Match the sentence parts. Put the right number in the box.

1 Map the task carefully

2 Start with scenic reading

3 Establish who the characters are

4 Consider how

5 Analyse the way characters speak

6 Examine the way the place

7 Focus on the action

8 Remember to

9 Highlight key words in the text

10 Make good use of these quotes

☐ A and the effect it has on the characters – and the audience. What causes it? What is the result?

☐ B and/or the time setting influence the action/ atmosphere.

☐ C mention devices like sarcasm, dramatic irony, comic relief – and to give a personal response, if required.

☐ D by writing good quoting paragraphs with the TQE pattern: T = 'mini-thesis' • Q = quote • E = explanation.

☐ E by highlighting the command word and key words.

☐ F to discover the gist (main theme/message).

☐ G and the roles they play.

☐ H and choose appropriate quotes to support your analysis.

☐ I to create an emotional effect (speech type; e.g. soliloquy/ dialogue/register/particular words).

☐ J they react and interact with each other (feelings/relationships).

4 PRACTICE Use the tips to practise analysing extracts from plays you have worked with in class.

Connectives to use in essays (cf. p. 89, task 5c)

Addition

Chronology

Contrast

Causality

Similarity

Attitude

Exemplification

Summary

Timeline of US history (cf. p. 97, task 1)

c. 13,000 BC

1492

after 1600

by the 1770s

1773

1775–1783

4th July 1776

1787

1848 and 1845-1852

1861–1865

1865

1896

1924

1950s–60s

1963

2008

2013

2021

Textquellen

8–9 By Doreen Lawrence, © 2013 Guardian News & Media Ltd.; **13** Karin Neuburger, Neue Züricher Zeitung, 26.08.19, www.nzz.ch; **16–17** From The Interestings, © 2013 Meg Wolitzer; **20** Laura Naima Kabelka "So hatte ich mir das Ganze nicht vorgestellt", aus SPIEGEL.de, vom 05.10.2020; **22.1** From: www.thirdsectorproject.co.uk, Data from Department for Digital, Culture, Media and Sport, 2018; **22.2** Statistics from the UN Secretary-General's Youth Envoy report, 2015; **23.1** Danee McGuire, 2017, www.one.org; **24–25** Jeff Orlowski © 2020 Guardian News & Media Ltd.; **29** Autor(en): Pia Stenner, Verlag/Subverlag: Netzpolitik.org; CC-BY-SA-4.0 Lizenzbestimmungen: https://creativecommons.org/licenses/by-sa/4.0/legalcode; **32–33** Gordon Brown © 2020 Guardian News & Media Ltd.; **37** Sind die Deutschen die besseren Briten geworden? Jochen Buchsteiner 19.09.2020 © 2020 Alle Rechte vorbehalten. Frankfurter Allgemeine Zeitung GmbH, Frankfurt. Zur Verfügung gestellt vom Frankfurter Allgemeine Archiv; **40.Task 2 (Zitat 1+2)** 2020, Kat Devlin, Pew Research Center, Washington, D.C.; **40.Task 2 (Zitat 3)** Branwen Jeffreys, https://www.bbc.com/news, 27 February 2019; **42–43** Ben Wyatt © 2021 Guardian News & Media Ltd.; **47** © 2017, Hanna Lose, Selina Möhring, USATipps.net; **50-51** 2021, Deutsche Welthungerhilfe e. V. https://www.welthungerhilfe.de/hunger/; **52–53** Copyright © 2015 See-Saw Films, Screenplay "Lion" by Luke Davies, adapted from the autobiographic novel "A long way home" by Saroo Brierley; **57** Gerhard Richter, 18.06.2017, https://www.deutschlandfunkkultur.de; **60–61** „Am Ende der Straße", Frankfurter Allgemeine Sonntagszeitung, 9. Juni 2019, Arezu Weitholz © Alle Rechte vorbehalten. Frankfurter Allgemeine Zeitung GmbH, Frankfurt. Zur Verfügung gestellt vom Frankfurter Allgemeine Archiv; **62–63** Jacob Mikanowski. ©2018 Guardian News & Media Ltd.; **67–68** Uwe Jean Heuser, https://www.zeit.de/2020/23/globalisierung-corona-wirtschaftskrise-nationen-wohlstand-pandemie 27. Mai 2020; **72-73** Excerpts from „Echo Boy" by Matt Haig, The Bodley Head, an imprint of Random House Children's Publishers UK, part of The Random House Group Ltd, London, 2014; **76–77** Julia Lorenz, „Hundert Augen": Überwachen und kuscheln, 31.08.20, taz.de; **78** Stevie Shephard © 2019 BBC, https://www.bbcgoodfood.com; **79** Robin McKie © 2019 Guardian News & Media Ltd.; **80-81** Peter James © 2021 Guardian News & Media Ltd.; **85** „Fragmente der Trauer" zuerst erschienen in der Frankfurter Allgemeinen Zeitung vom 08.09.2020, S. 11, von Kevin Hanschke © Alle Rechte vorbehalten. Frankfurter Allgemeine Zeitung GmbH, Frankfurt. Zur Verfügung gestellt vom Frankfurter Allgemeine Archiv; **87.Zitat 1** © 2018 Mark Bradley, https://yubasutterarts.org/; **87.Zitat 2** © 2018 Mark Bradley, https://yubasutterarts.org/; **108** Jonathan Freedland © 2021 Guardian News & Media Ltd.

*3 Lizenzbestimmungen zu CC-BY-SA-4.0 siehe: http://creativecommons.org/licenses/by-sa/4.0/legalcode

Bildquellen

Cover.1 plainpicture GmbH & Co. KG RF, Hamburg (DEEPOL by plainpicture/Bonfanti Diego); **Cover.2** Getty Images Plus, München (iStock / Wittayayut); **11.1** ShutterStock.com RF, New York (pikselstock); **11.2** Alamy stock photo, Abingdon (Janine Wiedel Photolibrary); **11.3** ShutterStock.com RF, New York (Diego Cervo); **11.4** ShutterStock.com RF, New York (LightField Studios); **14.1** ShutterStock.com RF, New York (Digital Storm); **14.2** 123rf Germany, c/o Inmagine GmbH, Nidderau (Radek Procyk); **14.3** ShutterStock.com RF, New York (Arthimedes); **14.4** ShutterStock.com RF, New York (ProStockStudio); **18.1** PhotoAlto, Paris; **21.1** stock.adobe.com, Dublin (Phongsak); **22.1** 123rf Germany, c/o Inmagine GmbH, Nidderau (dolgachov); **22.2** ShutterStock.com RF, New York (Shawn Goldberg); **23.1** Getty Images Plus, München (Image Source); **23.2** Getty Images Plus, München (SDI Productions); **26.1** stock.adobe.com, Dublin (Damir Khabirov); **26.2** ShutterStock.com RF, New York (M-SUR); **27.1** ShutterStock.com RF, New York (MJTH); **27.2** stock.adobe.com, Dublin (Daniel Ernst); **30.1** CartoonStock Ltd, Bath (Kelly Kincaid); **30.2** CartoonStock Ltd, Bath (William Haefeli); **31.1** stock.adobe.com, Dublin (shocky); **31.2** stock.adobe.com, Dublin (highwaystarz); **32.1** Getty Images, München (Mike Kemp); **32.2** ShutterStock.com RF, New York (Elena Rostunova); **36.1** ShutterStock.com RF, New York (cktravels.com); **37.1** Alamy stock photo, Abingdon (Tony Smith); **38.1** www.CartoonStock.com, Bath (Ed Fischer); **38.2** ShutterStock.com RF, New York (loocmill); **38.3** www.CartoonStock.com, Bath (McKeough, Joe); **38.4** Alamy stock photo, Abingdon (marc zakian); **39.1** Getty Images Plus, München (Christopher Ames); **39.2** Getty Images Plus, München (Ian Dyball); **40.1** www.CartoonStock.com, Bath (Love, Jason); **40.2** www.CartoonStock.com, Bath (BART); **40.3** Source: ec.europa.eu/eurostat; **41.1** stock.adobe.com, Dublin (FS-Stock); **41.2** Alamy stock photo, Abingdon (Angelo Andreas Zinna); **41.3** stock.adobe.com, Dublin (NicoElNino); **41.4** stock.adobe.com, Dublin (Seventyfour); **42.1** Getty Images, München (Keystone-France); **42.2** ShutterStock.com RF, New York (Linda Parton); **44.1** ShutterStock.com RF, New York (Asatur Yesayants); **44.2** ShutterStock.com RF, New York (Romain Biard); **44.3** Alamy stock photo, Abingdon (Granger Historical Picture Archive); **46.1** Alamy stock photo, Abingdon (Action Plus Sports Images); **48.1** CartoonStock Ltd, Bath (Paul Fell); **48.2** CartoonStock Ltd, Bath (Ron Hauge); **48.3** CartoonStock Ltd, Bath (Tom Toro); **48.4** www.CartoonStock.com, Bath (Christ Wildt); **49.1** Media Office GmbH, Kornwestheim/nach: Pew Research Center, 2020; **50.1** ShutterStock.com RF, New York (Agarianna76); **51.1** www.CartoonStock.com, Bath (Mischa Richter); **51.2** ShutterStock.com RF, New York (Alba_alioth); **52.1** Alamy stock photo, Abingdon (Fredrik Renander); **55.1** ShutterStock.com RF, New York (Rangeecha); **55.2** ShutterStock.com RF, New York (Craig Dingle); **58.1** ShutterStock.com RF, New York (CherylRamalho); **58.2** ShutterStock.com RF, New York (Rinku Dua); **58.3** ShutterStock.com RF, New York (kev Hughes); **58.4** ShutterStock.com RF, New York (Machekhin Evgenii); **59.1** Getty Images Plus, München (Martin Harvey); **59.2** ShutterStock.com RF, New York (Chinkub); **59.3** stock.adobe.com, Dublin (Kzenon); **59.4** Alamy Stock Photo, Abingdon, Oxon (Pascal Mannaerts); **59.5** ShutterStock.com RF, New York (Finn stock); **59.6** iStockphoto, Calgary, Alberta (chudesign); **62.1** ShutterStock.com RF, New York (Inspiring); **64.1** iStockphoto, Calgary, Alberta (Groomee); **64.2** Getty Images Plus, München (SolStock); **65.1** Media Office GmbH, Kornwestheim; **69.1** WWF Deutschland, Jahresbericht 2018/2019, 2020; **69.2** Oxfam international, Annual report 2018-2019, 2020; **69.3** Statista GmbH, Hamburg; **69.3** Media Office GmbH, Kornwestheim ; Statista GmbH, Hamburg; (Finanzielle Unterstützung einer NonProfit Organisation); **70.1** CartoonStock Ltd, Bath (Hawkins, Len); **70.2** CartoonStock Ltd, Bath (Boughen, Brendan); **71.1** stock.adobe.com, Dublin (dusk); **71.2** stock.adobe.com, Dublin (smile23); **72.1** ShutterStock.com RF, New York (vs148); **74.1** ShutterStock.com RF, New York (ALDECA studio); **74.2** ShutterStock.com RF, New York (Creations); **78.1** www.CartoonStock.com, Bath (Kamagurka); **79.1** CartoonStock Ltd, Bath (Gross, Sam); **80.1** Alamy stock photo, Abingdon (The National Trust Photolibrary); **80.2** Alamy stock photo, Abingdon (Geraint Lewis); **82.1** Alamy stock photo, Abingdon (Imageplotter); **82.2** Alamy stock photo, Abingdon (Donald Cooper); **82.3** Alamy stock photo, Abingdon (PA Images); **83.1** Alamy stock photo, Abingdon (Gordon Scammell); **83.2** Alamy stock photo, Abingdon (Geraint Lewis); **84.1** Getty Images, München (s: Andrea Pistolesi); **86.1** www.CartoonStock.com, Bath (Trevor Spaulding); **86.2** www.CartoonStock.com, Bath (Maria Scrivan); **86.3** www.CartoonStock.com, Bath (Rob Murray); **86.4** www.CartoonStock.com, Bath (Lee Lorenz); **87.1** (c) Royal Shakespeare Company; **87.2** © Royal Shakespeare Company; **89.1** stock.adobe.com, Dublin (Gstudio); **90.1** www.CartoonStock.com, Bath (Mike Flanagan); **91.1** www.CartoonStock.com, Bath (Jody Zellman); **92.1** ShutterStock.com RF, New York (Michal Urbanek); **103.1** Alamy stock photo, Abingdon (Mike Grandmaison / All Canada Photos); **103.2** stock.adobe.com, Dublin (Achim Thomae);